# Sex, Shamanism, and Healing:
# My Kissing Quest

BY

KATIE WEATHERUP

*A Hands over Heart Publishing book*

SEX, SHAMANISM, AND HEALING: MY KISSING QUEST
Copyright © 2019 by Katie Weatherup

All rights reserved.

Printed in the United States of America. No part of this book may be used or reproduced in any manner whatsoever without written permission from Katie Weatherup, except in the case of brief quotations in critical articles and reviews.

Second Edition

First Printing

August 2019

Cover Design by Jennifer Masters

Editing by Mara Clear Spring and Laura Kate Barrett

Book layout and text design by Laura Kate Barrett

ISBN 978-0-9778154-7-0

# TABLE OF CONTENTS

### INTRODUCTION ........................................................................................... 1
- *Welcome.................................................................................................. 1*
- *Finding a roadmap................................................................................. 1*
- *How this book began.............................................................................. 2*
- *My best hopes and wishes....................................................................... 2*
- *A word on perspective............................................................................ 3*

### CHAPTER 1—THE QUEST ............................................................................ 5
- *"I've not been kissed enough today. Could you help me with that?"..... 5*
- *The playing field: Safety and security ................................................. 10*
- *Behind the quest: Healing early negative experiences........................ 11*
- *Soul retrieval: Putting ourselves together again................................. 13*

### CHAPTER 2—RESPONSES, REJECTIONS, AND REACTIONS........................ 15
- *More general responses ....................................................................... 19*
- *The desire for attention ....................................................................... 21*
- *Negative reactions ............................................................................... 24*

### CHAPTER 3—EXPLORING SEX .................................................................. 25
- *Almost "there"..................................................................................... 25*
- *Even closer........................................................................................... 26*
- *A cosmic curveball............................................................................... 27*
- *...And then a healing ........................................................................... 29*
- *Test # 1................................................................................................. 29*
- *Test # 2................................................................................................. 31*
- *Finding what fits .................................................................................. 31*
- *The love hormone................................................................................. 33*

### CHAPTER 4—ATTRACTION....................................................................... 34
- *Who we attract or feel attraction for.................................................... 34*
- *Wanting the wrong type of partner...................................................... 35*
- *When the wrong partner wants you..................................................... 36*
- *Not interested at all—"I don't feel sexy" ............................................ 36*

### CHAPTER 5—EMBRACING WHAT IS......................................................... 39
- *Living with our shadow ....................................................................... 40*
- *The lessons of infidelity ....................................................................... 42*
- *Embracing the past .............................................................................. 43*
- *A new perspective ................................................................................ 46*
- *Honoring what is ................................................................................. 48*

### CHAPTER 6—SEXUAL HEALING ............................................................... 50
- *The truth of sex.................................................................................... 51*
- *Sex teaches one to be present............................................................... 52*
- *Listening to our own wisdom ............................................................... 54*
- *Emotional pressure cooker................................................................... 55*
- *Kindness heals...................................................................................... 56*
- *The pain of healing .............................................................................. 57*
- *Learning your own boundaries............................................................ 60*

### CHAPTER 7—TOUCH AND SEX ................................................................. 62
- *Learning how I wanted to be touched ................................................. 63*

- *The effects of molestation*.................................................. 64
- *Enjoying non-sexual touch*................................................. 64
- *Humans need touch—every day!* ....................................... 66
- CHAPTER 8—BETWEEN WOMEN ........................................... 68
  - *Hidden prejudice* .............................................................. 69
  - *Healing the wounds between women* ................................ 70
  - *Healing negative self image* .............................................. 72
  - *Opening your heart*........................................................... 73
- CHAPTER 9—ENJOYING THE DELIGHTFUL MASCULINE ............. 75
  - *Misleading stereotypes*...................................................... 76
  - *How men connect* ............................................................. 76
  - *The wounded and/or unavailable man*............................... 77
  - *Signs of pleasure* .............................................................. 78
  - *What a man wants* ........................................................... 80
  - *Enjoy receiving from the masculine*................................... 81
  - *Feeling attractive and safe*................................................ 82
  - *You are attractive—believe it!*........................................... 83
- CHAPTER 10—DEALING WITH UNCOMFORTABLE FEELINGS ABOUT MEN ..... 86
  - *Recognizing old patterns*................................................... 87
  - *Recognizing others' pain* .................................................. 88
  - *Going into your fears*........................................................ 89
  - *Why we believe these stories*............................................. 90
  - *Making a change* .............................................................. 91
- CHAPTER 11—NAVIGATING CONNECTIONS WITH MEN ............. 94
  - *Finding intelligent compassion* ......................................... 95
  - *Trust your intuition*........................................................... 95
  - *Develop a personal scale* .................................................. 97
  - *Opening to men* ................................................................ 97
- CHAPTER 12—THE OUCHY STUFF ........................................... 99
  - *Veils of separation*............................................................ 99
  - *Letting go and trusting*.................................................... 101
  - *Resisting intimacy and relationships* ............................... 102
  - *Come back to yourself*..................................................... 103
  - *What do you want?* ......................................................... 104
  - *What is your pattern?* ..................................................... 105
  - *Discernment* ................................................................... 106
  - *Anger*............................................................................. 107
  - *Pain* ............................................................................... 108
  - *The rewards*.................................................................... 110
- CHAPTER 13—THE SHAMANIC PERSPECTIVE........................... 111
  - *Past life connections*....................................................... 113
  - *How like attracts like* ...................................................... 114
  - *And so shamanic practice!* .............................................. 115
  - *Destiny path energy*........................................................ 116
  - *Watch out for that turn*.................................................... 117
  - *Interpersonal transmutation*............................................ 120

## Chapter 14—Shamanic Healing of Sexuality ... 121
*Reiki treatments ... 121*
*Additional treatment options ... 122*
*Soul retrieval ... 123*
*How we lose soul pieces ... 123*
*Soul retrieval for healing sexuality ... 125*
*Victim/Perpetrator relationships ... 126*
*No time in shamanic reality ... 127*

## Chapter 15—Masculine and Feminine Energies ... 129
*Yin + yang = all of us ... 129*
*Balancing yin & yang aspects ... 130*
*Shamanic journey for the feminine/masculine balance ... 131*
*Yin/yang manifestation techniques ... 132*
*I want! The yin approach ... 133*
*Cleaning house ... 133*
*Mixing yin and yang styles for manifestation ... 134*
*Recognizing your personal blend of feminine/masculine energies ... 135*

## Chapter 16—Meeting the Masculine Divine ... 136
*A message from Pele ... 136*
*Making love to the divine masculine ... 137*
*A divine father figure ... 139*
*Meeting the masculine warriors ... 139*
*Women healing men? ... 141*
*Men's sacred space ... 141*
*Ancient wisdom for modern men ... 142*
*Men's club—members only!?! ... 142*
*A cave experience in Hawaii ... 143*
*Healing for the guardian ... 143*
*Many flavors of the masculine ... 145*

## Chapter 17—The Healing Process ... 146
*Healing for the Physical, Energetic and Soul levels ... 147*
*Working on the appropriate level ... 149*
*When everything aligns ... 150*

## Chapter 18—How to Deal with Strong Emotion ... 151
*Some techniques ... 151*
*When strong emotions are combined with trauma ... 152*
*Tenderness towards the self ... 153*
*Additional tools ... 154*
*Being in your body ... 154*
*Taking action ... 155*

## Chapter 19—Exercises: Connecting with Spirit Guides and Archetypes . 157
*Inviting spirit guides ... 157*
*Meeting your goddess guide ... 158*
*Meeting Pele ... 161*
*Connecting with the masculine divine ... 161*
*Inviting in a power animal ... 161*

*Exercises* .................................................................................................. *162*
*Preparation* .............................................................................................. *163*
*Roots into the ground* ............................................................................ *163*
*Adding on layers to the root visualization* ........................................ *164*
*Meditation/Shamanic journey to connect with your inner child* ...... *165*
*Create a sacred vessel* ........................................................................... *167*
*Reconciling the masculine and feminine within* ............................... *167*
*Take it a step further* .............................................................................. *168*
*Balancing the masculine and feminine energies* ............................... *169*
*More visualizations* ................................................................................ *170*
*Eighth chakra* .......................................................................................... *170*
*Opening and clearing the chakras* ....................................................... *170*
*Healing through movement* ................................................................... *171*
*Specifically moving sexual energy* ...................................................... *172*
*Tantra work* .............................................................................................. *173*
CHAPTER 20—ALONG MY PERSONAL JOURNEY ................................ 176
*Finding soul truth* ................................................................................... *176*
*Healing Journey* ...................................................................................... *179*
*Men heal from proximity* ....................................................................... *181*
IN CONCLUSION ............................................................................................ 184

BIBLIOGRAPHY/RECOMMENDED READING ........................................... 187
HEALING PRACTITIONERS AND OTHER RESOURSES ............................... 190
CLASSES AND WORKSHOPS ...................................................................... 191

For Laura Kate Barrett, because she helps me laugh, grow, and believe in myself. She has been and remains a wise woman, a teacher, a partner in crime, an instigator, a cheerleader, and a beloved friend. My life is immeasurably richer for her friendship.

# INTRODUCTION

## Welcome…
This book is a kiss and tell. It tells my stories of fun, juicy, sexual experiences; long, sweet kisses; whispered words and touches in the dark; all offering the reader a vicarious experience.

This book is a roadmap to healing for survivors of sexual trauma. It offers new routes, pathways, and wisdom to make that journey swifter, more pleasurable, and more complete than the conventional routes alone.

This book is a guide to women's empowerment, to finding, embracing, and actualizing the feminine divine within. It's a journey to finding and joyfully claiming your power, complete with detailed exercises and instructions.

This book is an opening to healing between men and women. It offers ways to bridge the gap between the sexes and to open to a balance in which both are empowered, honored, healed.

This book is an invitation. Come and play with me.

## Finding a roadmap
Sexual energy is rich, juicy, and life affirming. It pains me that so many people have shut it down, feel shame about it, or treat it like an itch to be scratched. Disowning sexual energy is to the energetic being and psyche much like the loss of an arm or a leg would be to the physical

being. Embracing that aspect of self is a primal part of a rich and good relationship to oneself.

Yet we seem to lack good roadmaps for finding our way to our sexuality. So much of the discourse on the subject is about who is doing it wrong or badly. Our sexual dialogue is often degraded to the lowest common denominator of marketing and dire cautionary tales.

This book is meant to provide a roadmap or at least an example of a journey to empowered sexuality that is as much fun as the sexual energy itself. Given that sexual energy is juicy, rich, and fun, shouldn't the journey there also include those attributes? Furthermore, the journey should be customized, made personal, so that each traveler feels safe and is meeting this energy at exactly the level they are prepared to experience.

## How this book began

This book began following a conversation with a dear friend. She had started me on my kissing quest a few years before and I commented that while I felt done with my kissing quest, it was such a great and empowering idea that it should surely be shared. She suggested that this could be my next book.

Upon further consideration, I realized that much of the shamanic work that I do relates to healing wounds around sexuality. I work with a number of women who have experienced sexual trauma, and I've developed skills with my shamanic work to assist with an accelerated and transformational healing process. This book allows me to share the knowledge I have collected.

Part of my reason for writing this book relates simply to the fun factor. I love talking about sexuality and my kissing quest. I thrive on hearing about joyful sexual experiences from other people. So, this book has been fun to write, fun to talk about, and is fun, I hope, to read.

## My best hopes and wishes

One night when I was working on my book, I went outside and prayed to spirit. I was feeling as though my perspective was too narrow, that my words were unclear, that in striving for a middle road people would find that my book either moved too quickly or was too simplistic to help them.

In my prayers, I clarified my best hopes and wishes for the book. I see that there is great pain that people cause themselves with their stories around sexuality and relationships. I see men and women, who want most to be loved by the other, misinterpret one another and create pain rather than pleasure. Women especially make themselves wrong for desiring expression of their sexuality and feelings, and thus set aside pieces of themselves.

So much avoidable suffering happens in relationships, both in the relationship to self and the relationship to one's lover. In my shamanic work, I clear away old pain, damage, and darkness, transmuting these energies back to pure universal life-force energy. My deepest hope and prayer for this book is that the words and ideas will help heal the pain that arises in relationships and around sexuality.

## A word on perspective

One of the limitations of this book is that it's mostly about heterosexual relationships. While there is a great deal of information men may find valuable, the examples and much of the writing are oriented towards women, specifically straight or bisexual women. Most of my clients and students are women, so this is the experience I am drawing from as a teacher and practitioner. As of the writing of this book, I simply haven't had enough experience of being with women sexually to write extensively about it. My bisexuality is still fairly new territory and while I talk about it a bit, overall I just don't have enough data to feel qualified drawing extensive conclusions. It is not my intent to disregard anyone's sexuality. Only that this book is a very personal journey and I have made the choice to only write what I know.

In that vein, when I talk about shamanism, I am talking about one way or one framework for understanding the unseen world. There are many other equally valid stories, allegories, ideas, and frameworks to conceptualize the vast, unknowable mystery of the universe and the

Divine. You don't have to believe in spirit guides or my framework in order to benefit from the ideas in this book. In fact, I invite you to disregard whatever part of my framework, ideas, or suggestions don't fit for you.

As I prepare to send this book out into the world, I'm aware of the feelings of vulnerability that arise, especially given how transparent I have elected to make my sexual experience. Most people will likely disagree with some of what I've written. My intent is not to write a book that is objective truth for everyone. Rather, in sharing my personal truth, I hope to plant seeds, offer new ideas, and suggest pathways to greater peace and healing. So, again, I invite you to take what serves and leave the rest. Whatever use you make of it, thank you for taking the time to open my book.

# Chapter 1—The Quest

"I've not been kissed enough today. Could you help me with that?"

With these words I created a powerful journey of self-knowledge by way of sensual delight, one that I still remember fondly, years later. At 27, nearly a year after I had left my first lover (whom I had been with for seven years), I realized that I had only kissed five men, total. I had the challenge of having had very little sexual experience and no clear picture of how to proceed into that shadowy land of flirting and dating. It was disheartening to feel so far behind the curve in the sexual area, since I had a proven record as an overachiever in other areas of my life.

In the year after that relationship ended, when faced with a man I was even a little bit attracted to, I tended to blush and stutter. I've never been good at small talk and talking to men brought back the worst moments of my junior-high shyness. Men who were interested in me would ask me several questions, which I would answer as briefly as possible. The ability to then ask them a question or offer a conversational gambit was beyond me. I was hopelessly, painfully shy around attractive members of the opposite sex.

This meant that the usual approach of meeting and dating men was simply setting the bar a bit too high for me. I'm also not an especially patient person. I had just spent a year working through the ending of my relationship; I was ready to begin gathering more experience, and I wanted it now, damn it!

The problem was further compounded by the fact that I'm just not a big drinker. Many people who suffer from shyness have found that a judicious application of alcohol takes the edge off and allows them to loosen up. That didn't work for me. It's not a moral issue, but about being in control. I hate feeling out of control, so tequila was not going to be my dis-inhibitor of choice.

When a dear friend proposed the kissing quest, it satisfied all the needed criteria. It turned out, in retrospect, to be the beginning of a formative experience of self-discovery, in which I developed my discernment about sexual energy and began a powerful healing journey. My brilliant friend, mentor, and cheerleader came up with an idea that spoke to my engineering background and allowed me to play to my strengths: when meeting someone under the preferred conditions, skip the small talk and bring a compelling issue near and dear to my heart immediately into the conversation: my need to be kissed. My training as an engineer required me to develop creative solutions to problems, allowing them to be addressed with great efficiency. I saw no reason not to apply this skill set to acquiring the experience I desired.

My goal was to be kissed as often as possible. This gave me a chance to practice flirting skills and play with sexual energy in a nice, safe way. I would make it clear to the person of choice that I was only interested in exchanging a kiss with someone, not propositioning that person to share my bed. I would communicate my goal to be kissed in the clearest possible manner. After being kissed, I would say "Thank you" nicely, then turn and walk away. If anyone got confused and assumed it was personal, generally kissing two or three of the other men present would disabuse him of that notion.

As an intelligent, shy, bookish girl, I had, up to that point in my life, spent vastly more time reading about kisses than experiencing them. Plus, they look so great in the movies. So, come hell or high water, by the time I was finished with this quest, I knew I would have had the opportunity to thoroughly explore the kissing experience and have a good picture of what it's all about. The quest allowed me to go forward in my life, free from the feeling that there was some mythical, magical kissing experience that I had somehow missed out on.

The kissing quest was conducted in places where I felt safe and was surrounded by friends. I picked environments to play where people were likely to understand and enjoy my goals. The kissing would be indiscriminate. I wanted to entice men to come up and kiss me, so I would make it as safe as possible. Unless I had a compelling reason, I wouldn't turn anyone down. That meant that those who approached me and played with me didn't have to worry about being judged or evaluated. They could share a moment with me without fear of rejection.

It helped with the whole stammering thing, because I could easily get one pre-rehearsed line out—and if I gave the man something else to do with his mouth, he was unlikely to notice my inability to conduct a simple conversation!

The game suited on another level; it spoke to the part of me that has little time and patience for small talk, casual conversation, and shallow human connections. Part of why I'm terrible to this day at small talk is that if I'm going to connect with another person, I want to have a meaningful connection. As a healing practitioner, I'm aware how difficult meaningful intimacy is for many people to accept and enjoy. So, there was this huge gift in getting to share an intimate moment with so many people in a way most of them could accept.

I loved learning about all the ways that people kiss: from the brief peck, to the slow conversation of touching of tongues and lips, to the light sensation of teeth, to the passionate intensity of strong pressure. Some men listen better than others with their bodies. I could feel their attention on gauging my response and adjusting the kiss, deepening it slowly when they found me receptive. For these kisses, it seemed like the movement of lips and tongues just flowed in effortless coordination of mutual pleasure. Sometimes a man only wanted to give me a kiss in his own style. He would participate in the experience without paying much attention to my more subtle responses. Others listened to my body and energy, felt my responses and adapted. I got to have all these moments of sharing mutual, undivided attention with another human being.

As my confidence grew, I could adjust my request for the circumstance. For example, the following conversation often occurred, with variations on the choice of alcoholic beverage:

> Attractive man: Would you like to try some of my Scotch? It's thirty years old.
>
> Katie: Well, I'm not really drinking tonight, but I'd be delighted to taste it on your lips.

Alternately,

> Attractive man: What can I offer you to drink?
>
> Katie: I'm not drinking tonight.
>
> Attractive man: Are you sure? I can offer you lots of choices.
>
> Katie: Well, the thing is, I prefer not to mix my vices, and there are other vices that I'm choosing to sample tonight. You see, I've not been kissed enough.

This statement was especially effective when accompanied by a knowing smile and a deep breath that lifted my chest. In most cases, men who offered me a drink could be relied upon to promptly provide a satisfying kiss when asked.

I learned so much. For example, did you know that shy, sweet guys often kiss much better than the more confident ones? Men who weren't as confident were more likely to pay more attention to me and to treat the experience like a gift. Whether it's a conversation, a kiss, or a night in bed, I have vastly better experiences with men who treat the energy, attention, and sexuality that I share as a precious and wonderful gift. Guys who find it easy to get women into bed all too often have an unfortunate habit of being casual and careless with the gift of a woman's sexuality.

I discovered that, on average, women kiss better than men. I think it's because women do a better job of being present in the moment of a kiss. When I kissed a woman, she didn't seem to be thinking about whether she could grab my ass or get me into bed. She was just thinking about the kiss. It was a safe, pressure-free way for me to acknowledge my bisexuality without needing to take if further until I was ready.

I gained confidence in my own ability to arouse, please, and attract. Most of the men I kissed would have gladly kissed me again or explored further if I had allowed it. Having felt rather unattractive for much of my life, it was an amazing gift to feel assured in my sexual attractiveness. So many beautiful, desirable women feel unattractive. In walking mindfully through that territory, I had the chance to transform my self-image and learn how to help others do the same. Now, years later, I have put that knowledge forth for others to use in classes and this book.

Even when I felt complete with the kissing quest, or was involved with someone who didn't want me kissing lots of people, I could talk about it. For someone who is terrible at small talk, I've got to say it makes a great conversational gambit. Whether others saw me so or not, I had a great deal of self-consciousness around a history of being perceived as the dull, straight-laced, GoodyTwo-Shoes. Too many teachers and parents had asked my peers some form of the question, "Why can't you be more like Katie?" As you may imagine, I was not a girl who got invited to parties.

As time went by I simply became less shy. After asking a total stranger to kiss you out of the blue enough times, talking to a man simply gets less intimidating. I did find that my original calculation that I would only have to say one, pre-rehearsed thing was incorrect. More than half the time, I got asked to repeat myself. I do mumble and talk fast when I'm nervous, but I think this had more to do with the men just not quite believing I had said what it sounded like I had said.

## The playing field: Safety and security

One of the most important elements of the kissing quest was that timing and location were critical. For this to be fun and good and right for me, I needed to be completely safe at every moment. My goal was to minimize the risk of rejection and avoid all risk of actual physical danger or unpleasantness. I wouldn't, for example, try my kissing quest in a bar in downtown San Diego. I don't frequent bars; I get overwhelmed by the energy, so I don't understand the environment well enough to feel safe.

I found that the safest, most productive ground for my kissing quest was Society for Creative Anachronism (SCA). The SCA is a medieval recreation group. Unlike the Renaissance Pleasure Faire®, the SCA is a non-profit organization less for show and more for the people who want to play. Events can draw thousands or even as many as 10,000 in the case of one of hundreds of annual events. That's a lot of potentially kissable men! Add to that the titillation of getting that many grownups to play dress up with me. It is a great deal of fun.

In addition to the many delightful experiences the SCA has afforded me over the years, this sub-culture offered a uniquely friendly atmosphere for my kissing quest game and exploration. The culture is largely sex-positive, so much so that people sometimes claim SCA really stands for Society of Consenting Adults.

I've always been baffled by the misogynistic attitudes of some heterosexual men. Men tend to be seriously motivated by the desire for sex. Yet, when they impose punitive language and labels on women or hold them in contempt for being sexual, they limit their own supply. It is unappealing to share one's body with a man only to become less to him and his peers. I prefer for the response to the question, "Did you still respect her in the morning?" to be "I respected her one hell of a lot more in the morning!"

If women don't need to fear being labeled or judged, there's greater freedom to be expressive sexually. By and large, I found that within the SCA, my sexuality was met with unmitigated support and approval, however little or much I chose to express and share. The SCA is also a remarkably safe place to play physically. I was warned when I first entered the group not to yell for help unless I meant it, because I would have a huge number of armed men (and some women) rushing to my defense. I have walked around alone at 3 a.m., in a camp filled with drunken men, and felt totally safe. It's amazing to walk alone at night in a public place and not have to be alert for potential rapists in the bushes.

There's a great deal of power in spending time among men who, individually and collectively, feel a deep personal investment in the safety and comfort of the women around them. SCA members have told me over and over again how rape never happens in the Society. Whether that's completely true or not, I certainly have no direct evidence to the contrary, and I have seen men act quickly and decisively to address any situation where a woman might be made to feel uncomfortable.

Some might argue that the intensity and focus of the group on making sure the women—all women, all ages, all shapes and sizes—feel well protected and safe is condescending and sexist. However, I found it to be the perfect place to feel safe enough to finally let my sexual self grow and develop. Thousands of experiences of men going to some effort in large and small ways to ensure my comfort and well-being has been an amazing gift, allowing me to develop a deep trust in the fundamental goodness of the masculine.

## Behind the quest: Healing early negative experiences

The kissing quest was a journey of self-healing as well as self-knowledge. When I was five, I was molested by the father of a kindergarten friend. I was over at her house before school and her father got me alone, pulled down my pants and touched me. Then, he threatened to kill me or my parents (I don't remember which) if I told anyone. I spent the whole day at school sick, scared, shocked, trying to pretend to be normal, not knowing what to do, but sure that if I didn't hold it together, things would be much worse. I don't remember the moment with the man clearly, but I can remember that day in school.

Once I got home, my mom knew something was wrong and had the story out of me in about five minutes. My parents agreed that taking legal action would subject me to additional trauma and settled for informing the mother of my friend of what had happened, and life went on. I forgot all about it until much later.

As adult survivors of molestation, it can be hard to even wrap our minds around how our quality of life has been impacted. With adult sexual trauma, there is a before and after picture. Here's what my sexuality looked like before, here's where things are different—it gives us a good gauge for knowing when things are processed, healed, completed. It allows the survivor to know what works in that healing process, because with the things that work, the symptoms are reduced, the pain is less.

Childhood molestation causes damage that becomes incorporated into our experiences of sexuality. This overwhelming, awful "thing" happened and by the time we begin to know ourselves as sexual beings, that pain and wounding is simply part of the territory. There's no clear energetic reference for what clear, clean, unwounded sexuality feels like. Only when we arrive there do we learn what it feels like. The great news is that healing our sexuality can lead to delightful, empowering discoveries again and again as the pain is recognized, relieved, and cleared away. That path, à la kissing quest, can be rich and pleasurable territory.

Being the energetically sensitive person that I am, I grew up finding sexual energy tremendously threatening. The first time I felt sexual energy, it was bad, invasive, horrible, and scary. It was mixed with the molester's desire, self-loathing, and fear. I spent my childhood and adolescence being negatively reactive to men. If I was alone with a man, I was on red-alert, hyper-aware of feeling unsafe, while desperately trying to maintain my composure and pretend I wasn't so frightened.

I developed very large breasts very early, and while the adult men in my life were appropriate in terms of behavior, they were still noticing me sexually. As a pre-teen and a teenager, there was a fairly constant bombardment of juvenile sexual attention directed my way. I shut down and felt overwhelmed by this energy.

When I was older, my mother told me about the molestation, but it felt like something that had happened to someone else. I didn't even remember it; it couldn't possibly have affected me! Still, when I heard about a practice called soul retrieval, I knew instinctively how important it was for me to have this healing. Some part of me knew I needed this work in order to have all of me come home to myself again.

## Soul retrieval: Putting ourselves together again

The idea behind soul retrieval is that when we go through trauma, part of our awareness and being leaves to avoid being wounded. Psychologists call this dissociation; shamanic folks refer to it as soul loss. We can leave parts of our energy behind in relationships and through things like surgery and car accidents. But of all life experiences, sexual trauma seems, on average, to produce the most soul loss. The shamanic practice of soul retrieval deals with this directly, tracking and returning the lost energy and pieces, restoring wholeness and personal power.

When I had my soul retrieval and got the piece that separated during the molestation, along with the memory there was actually a huge sense of relief. I suddenly understood why I had always felt scared when I was alone with my mother's friends' husbands. I understood why I tended to shut down sexually and avoid that territory. It was a huge relief to know that my own craziness about sexuality actually made perfect sense; it wasn't that there was something wrong with me, just some wounds to be healed. The timing was perfectly aligned with my original plan to assist my frustratingly shy self by embarking upon the kissing quest.

The kissing quest was begun before my soul retrieval, another way I instinctively reached towards wholeness, custom tailored to my needs. It allowed me to begin to enjoy and feel safe around sexual energy. Because I was only exchanging a kiss, not going to bed with someone, the sexually charged energy remained at a distinct but manageable level.

I could feel into different types of encounters and experiences and note what felt good and what didn't. I made a point of kissing everyone who asked, unless I had a compelling reason not to—they were too drunk to stand up, sick, etc. Kissing the people who were less attractive to me had an empowering aspect. I could demonstrate to myself that I was still safe in a sexual situation. It helped me learn not to be overwhelmed by the random, uninvited, sexual attention that women experience. I can now say that it's just energy and only let through what I choose to accept. This is way more fun than hiding, staying home, and avoiding situations where men might randomly find me sexually desirable (like the supermarket).

Furthermore, even though I didn't enjoy being rejected, when someone turned down my invitation for a kiss, there was an aspect of empowerment. Men who were making passes at me and then fled when I asked for a kiss were fun in a way. I had suddenly turned the tables (although I wasn't thinking in those terms at the time) and become the sexual initiator rather than the passive receiver of their sexual attention. I was empowered in my sexuality instead of objectified. This process of empowerment has led me to realize so many gifts in my life, truths in my personal relationships, and tools in my shamanic practice. The kissing quest was a remarkable starting point on a path I still travel today.

# Chapter 2—Responses, Rejections, and Reactions

When I presented my dilemma to a potential participant in my quest—that I was far below my quota of kisses for the day—I typically was met with one of three responses:

**Inability to Cope:** Not being one to court rejection, I preferred to ask men who had spent time staring at me (or my breasts), going out of their way to catch my eye, or flirting with me—but I still got turned down by some of them! Was it alarming and upsetting to them to have the role of sexual initiator suddenly taken away? They blanched, fled, and complained. Some men were all about trying to attract my sexual attention, but they wanted any interaction to be on their terms.

**Uneasy Intrigue:** A second common reaction was one of intrigued alarm. Genuinely interested men were sometimes not sure what to do when I invited them to kiss me. It was exciting and scary all at the same time. These men generally worked their way around to kissing me, but first wanted to talk to me, perhaps to convince themselves I was serious or gather up the courage to break this social taboo. They seemed to find it an intense but intriguing energy.

**Unmitigated Pleasure**: The third reaction (and, of course, the most fun) was from the men who decided that I was the coolest woman they had ever met. They were delighted to kiss me, willing to provide any other attention I cared for, and wanted to watch as I kissed others. Some of them took great glee in explaining my quest to others, delighted to help me on my way.

The worst experience I had was with a man who managed to express all the trite and ridiculous ideas about women's sexuality. He was what you could call TFH—tall, fit, and handsome—and he was looking right at me, all good signs for a kiss. When a friend explained my quest to him, his first response was to ask a passive/aggressive question: if I had just kissed someone else, and then kissed him, wouldn't it be like he was kissing the man who had just kissed me?

I shrugged and started to walk away, yet he urged me to come back and indicated he'd like to kiss me. He said he had been at sea for a long time and just before he put his lips on mine, he whispered that he'd been waiting for this for a long time. Then he kissed me. It sounds like it would be charming, romance novel material, right? It wasn't. It wasn't that he had bad breath or a poor technique, but it felt icky. I didn't like it. So, after the kiss, I stepped back to walk away. The chivalrous Mr. TFH then complained that I couldn't rev him up and leave him standing. The look on my face must have told him he'd gone too far, for he caught my hand, kissed it sweetly and apologized, then allowed me to walk away without further complaint.

Once I left the revelry of that busy party, I realized what had felt unpleasant about the whole experience. Being in his presence brought me into the awareness of his belief system about women, which contained elements of misogyny and entitlement. This man was striving to obtain some access to my sexuality, while simultaneously identifying me as less desirable because I was being sexual with other men. He acted as if exchanging a kiss, even though he'd seen me kiss and walk away from other men, entitled him to full access to whatever he desired. Somehow he thought he could make his arousal and erection my problem.

It left a bad taste in my mouth, no pun intended. In the moment, it wasn't something that I thought through or analyzed. My body simply knew that the energy coming off of him was icky. It didn't feel safe or fun, no matter how pretty he was. That was something my kissing quest taught me, that I didn't need to overuse my brain figuring things out—my body would know if I was having fun or not as the energy flew around.

Lest this sound discouraging, here's one of my favorite kisses from early into my kissing quest: My aforementioned friend, mentor, and kissing quest inspiration took me out to a "juke joint" in Florida. Musicians and music lovers gather inside to enjoy the sounds. Between sets, we ventured outdoors around a big bonfire under huge, old live oak trees draped with Spanish moss, enjoying the sounds, the fire, and the stars. Music has been played there for decades by some of the most famous blues musicians.

That night the band was playing and we were dancing. I had the delightful experience of having several members of the band watching me as I felt the flow of taking in the music and radiating back my enjoyment and delight. Singing in a band for many years gave me a tremendous sense of the conscious energy exchange between the audience and the performers. An engaged, happy audience exudes energy back to the performers in a continuous loop; everyone enjoys a little energetic "high."

I especially connected energetically with one of the guitar players. Every time they took a break, he would come over and talk to me and my friend, offering to buy us a drink, play a song we'd like, or just to say hi. I, true to form, blushed and stammered, leaving my friend to carry the conversation. At the end of the night, I got up the courage to inform him that I hadn't been kissed today and to ask for his help. He made me repeat myself, sure that he hadn't heard me properly. Then he kissed me.

The man could kiss. He was already pretty entranced with me, and later spoke of watching me dance to the music he was making, and of playing only for me. The energy of his attraction to me and his delight at unexpectedly finding me in his arms came through in the touch of his lips and the taste of his tongue. It was, of course, marvelous.

I emailed him after I got back to California. We corresponded for a few years, and he wrote lovely things about my energy, the light in my eyes, how compelling and beautiful I was. It was a delightful experience all the way around; energetically fun, arousing, deeply flattering, and empowering. The man already thought I was attractive and exciting, but after my request for a kiss I went up to absolutely amazing in his esteem. In that moment when I asked him to kiss me, I had the chance to move from shy, blushing girl to direct and empowered woman.

The most amusing story related to a fellow who introduced himself as Romeo. He swaggered up to me and said, "Hi, I'm Romeo." I smiled up at him and said, "Hi, Romeo, I haven't been kissed enough tonight. Could you help me with that?" He began to stutter and look around frantically for something with which to occupy himself other than kissing me. One of my friends suggested that perhaps he needed a demonstration and promptly kissed me quite thoroughly. By the time I looked up, Romeo had fled. Our paths crossed a few more times that evening, and each time he made absolutely sure that there were as many people between us as possible so I couldn't talk directly to him. Apparently, he was a "Wherefore art thou?" kind of Romeo!

Amusement at Romeo's expense aside, one of the things I realized was, rather than holding all the cards in sexuality, men are often as confused and intimidated by sexual energy as women. Just as I was choosing my sexual playground very carefully in order to feel emotionally and energetically safe, the men were doing the same.

There was a bit of an unconscious bait and switch aspect to my appearance versus my purpose. Some men were drawn to me because I naturally give off the shy vibe. They felt that they could approach and initiate at their own pace, feel their way slowly, and back away if rejected. They weren't approaching the sexual, confident women, but the shy, demure ones. To have me suddenly ask to be kissed was like a bunny suddenly growing fangs, à la Monty Python.

One of the things I found interesting about some of the men who did celebrate and delight in my kissing quest was that sometimes it wasn't personal, not about me at all. Just as a man who backed away from his initial attraction when asked for a kiss wasn't fleeing from me personally but from an overwhelming situation, some of the men I talked to felt delighted to see a woman expressing sexuality in this fashion. Without having an agenda to take me home or talk me into bed, it seemed delightful and refreshing to them to see a woman playing with sexual energy in this fashion.

## More general responses

As I talked to friends, male and female, about the kissing quest, I was surprised at the range of responses.

For me, the kissing quest represented joyful, safe, wholesome, sexual fun. It was a way to play with the energy of sexuality with integrity that was safe for me. Plus, it gave me something to talk about that was a little racy. I was genuinely surprised to find that it pushed buttons for a lot of people.

Within my social circles, I often felt like the least adventurous person present. My sexual experience seemed so much less than that of my peers. So, it was truly a shock to have some people respond negatively to my quest and look upon me as somehow slutty or promiscuous.

I received a lot of comments from other women in tones of disbelief, "You'll kiss *anybody*?!?" or "But you'll catch herpes." (I didn't, by the way.) Some women reacted in a way that indicated that they found the whole thing distasteful. Others were fascinated. They knew it wasn't something that fit for them, personally, but they admired me for doing it and were delighted to have the vicarious experience. And for others it was a blend of both.

Much has been written about the Madonna/Whore dichotomy. This term is a useful, short-hand way to allude to the mixed messages about sexuality and the roles and labels assigned to women. The Madonna is the good girl, sexually chaste. She is the mother, the wife, the caretaker, the angel in the home. Also known as the nice girl or the lady, the Madonna resides on a pedestal and never gets invited to the good parties (she wouldn't want to go, now, would she?). For these pure, tame women, our society asserts that they should be protected and safe from male violence toward women.

The Whore, on the other hand, is the promiscuous woman. She's sexually active and available. She attracts lots of male attention, but by virtue of her role, society often considers her to have relinquished the right to protection and safety from male violence. If she is raped, well, some people would say that is expected given how she is, a terrible thing of course, but also her own fault on some level. She may be a target of misogyny from the same men who are vying for a place in her bed. The whore or slut has freedom of movement and attention for the bargain price of being judged and condemned. Women are treated differently by both sexes depending upon which category they appear to fit.

My kissing quest was especially gratifying to me because I defied those categories, being neither Madonna nor Whore. I learned a lot about myself. I found that I really don't like being in either category. If I felt like I was being placed in the "good girl" role, I would strive to show I was more interesting and sexual than that. When I perceived I'd been judged as a possible "slut", I would feel compelled to prove how relatively chaste I was—after all, I wasn't having sex with these men. Yet, "ladies" certainly don't kiss unknown, random men. As a feminist who believes that it is no one's business but her own what a woman does with her body, it was interesting to find myself maneuvering to still fit into the good girl category that I was simultaneously trying to get myself out of.

Sex wasn't the goal of my quest: in addition to experience and personal healing, I wanted approval and attention, and what gave me that with one person resulted in condemnation from another. I found it especially interesting to note the stereotypes people accept about women expressing sexual energy. Somehow, by definition, a woman who is advertising herself as a sexual being, dressing in a way that shows off her body, or flirting with more than one man is considered to be somehow unhealthy, self-destructive, and/or insecure. I was extremely fortunate to spend time in the company of many people, men and women, who found this idea to be pure, unadulterated bullshit.

Once I relaxed enough to enjoy my quest, I realized that flirting often has little to do with a desire for sex. It has everything to do with playing with sexual energy, human connection, and attention. I enjoy the attention and the admiration, and return those gifts in full measure. Running this kind of energy also takes a lot of energy, so playing with it a few times a month is about the right dose for me these days. Making space for that experience as a regular, but not daily, part of my life is the most fulfilling balance.

## The desire for attention

How can anyone deny that the desire for pleasure, attention, and admiration is natural? Like any human need, if it is out of balance, it can cause grief in one's life. But to automatically assume that anyone who is enjoying being the center of attention is unhealthy is to ignore something fundamental about the nature of human beings. It infuriates me that women are especially condemned for having sexuality play a role in meeting this need.

Human beings thrive on feeling special, important, and admired. That need is part of what allows us to succeed as social creatures. Some people need and desire more of these experiences than others. This is part of the difference between introverts and extroverts. Neither is better or worse, just different.

We all have different strategies to seek this attention and approval that we desire. One woman might wear a low-cut, sexy dress and enjoy the approval, admiration, and attention that come from responses to her sexual attractiveness. Another woman might comment to a friend that the woman showing off her body must have low self-esteem, how sad for her. When the woman is commenting to her friend, she's seeking to be "right" about the woman in the sexy dress and presenting herself as better by demonstrating how she conforms more closely to the "Madonna" role. Perhaps this woman is playing the critic because she feels insecure as the woman in the sexy dress is getting more attention and admiration. The unkind and malicious comments may be a way for this woman to feel important and receive attention and admiration from her friend.

Perhaps the friend who is listening to the comments doesn't share the opinion that the woman in the sexy dress is somehow bad or immature or wrong. But, by listening and nodding, she has the attention and approval of her friend. I have certainly used nodding, listening, and validating, even when I didn't agree or enjoy the conversation, to get approval and feel safe. After all, if I have disagreed with someone about a nasty comment, they might focus their unpleasantness on me. So, I might have listened to feel important or safe or both.

If we're honest and introspective, we can generally find within ourselves a need and desire for admiration, attention, and approval. We can also probably find ways that we've made uncomfortable sacrifices to get these things—whether it was allowing someone to touch us, or listening to an offensive conversation and not speaking our truth. If we are on a path of healing and growth, this moment of introspection is likely to also reveal that as we heal and grow, we can obtain approval and attention without dishonoring some other part of ourselves.

Carolyn Myss, a spiritual author, talks about archetypes found within everyone, one of which she calls the Prostitute. To me, the Prostitute is the part of us that is in charge of meeting our need for attention and approval. This part negotiates prices with other people and the world. The more solid we are in ourselves, the closer we come to buying this attention and approval with something that we delight in expressing anyway. Then we are not wearing masks or trying to please, but simply delighting in life and delighting in the delight of those around us. The need is fed and we're being ourselves in all our glory. This happens to be the sexiest imaginable way to run sexual energy.

A non-sexual example of this relates to my love of teaching. I love teaching for a lot of reasons. It empowers people, for one thing. But I also love teaching because it feels wonderful to have the undivided attention of a room full of people who can't wait to hear what I'll say next. When I'm in the zone or the flow, I'm channeling the perfect information for the group and I sound wise, warm, funny, and generally great, and I get to be the center of attention, filled with confidence, doing something I love.

I know that how I appear in that moment has a great deal to do with bringing the light of the universe through my words and energy; it's not me, it's everyone. But the human part of me loves it, too. It feels great—being a channel for universal energy, sharing information that makes people healthier and more whole, and being appreciated for it. Because it feels so good, I teach with joy and energy and enthusiasm and delight.

There's a part of me that still has judgments about meeting my need for attention with teaching. I feel like I should be there only for my students and somehow egoless. Yet, I know that I am a vastly better teacher because I am enjoying myself on many different levels. I give more. The energy and attention that my students offer me with their appreciation is energy that I cycle right back into my class.

It is ideal to move through the world with a strong sense of liking oneself. If we don't feel a sense of self-love or unconditional friendliness towards ourselves, no amount of external approval can fill us up. Yet human beings generally come from a place of self-esteem as a mixed bag. We love ourselves and value ourselves and criticize ourselves and beat up on ourselves. We are our own worst critic and hopefully our own biggest fan. This balance changes from day to day.

The kinder we are to ourselves, the less intense the need and longing for approval becomes. If we are partly filling up that cup by valuing ourselves, our need for that from the outside becomes less urgent. Nevertheless, even with a totally full loving-cup and great self-esteem, approval and attention still feel good. In fact, when I'm feeling great about myself, filled with energy, I can enjoy and delight in attention and approval the most.

At its best, meeting the need for attention and approval is an energy exchange where both sides are being filled up and more energy is created, as when I'm teaching and my delight in the attention and enthusiasm of my students causes me to give more, or when I'm flirting with someone and I feel great and they feel great.

## Negative reactions

Some people will judge and condemn us no matter what we do. It's not personal. As we make our choices and show them to the world, we sometimes act as a mirror that reflects back to such people what isn't healed in them. When a person doesn't like the reflection, they tend to get mad at the mirror. For example, if I lack confidence and I meet someone who is very confident, I may detest them for having access to the part of themselves that I long for but haven't actualized yet. I may call them selfish, self-absorbed, and insensitive. I'm sure some witnesses of my quest in action may have entertained similar thoughts about me.

We can't keep people from judging us. However, the more we choose our path based on what feels good and right for us, the less we judge ourselves, and the better time we'll have with this reality. I don't like being judged, but the less I try to people-please, put on masks, and be seen a certain way, the more of my energy is home with myself to deal with the "ouch" when someone doesn't "like" me. Over the years, the less I try to please people, the more people find it pleasing to spend time with me.

## Chapter 3—Exploring sex

As I continued my kissing quest, I began to feel safer with sexual energy and the motivation to do more than kiss. I discussed this with a friend of mine who shared a piece of advice, given by a mother to her daughter. The mother said that it's not good to have sex with everyone, because you'd never have time for anything else, like earning a living, and there are health risks. She also said it's not good to have sex with no one, because there are fundamental needs that go unmet and other health risks. "So, somewhere between having sex with Everyone and No One is the right balance for you. Find where "there" is for you." Locating "there" for me flowed into the next phase of exploration that involved taking lovers and trying on different flavors of relationships. Over the years I developed an excellent selection criteria for what sort of lovers would best meet my needs.

One of the things I learned for myself was that I am best served to hold out for sex that is personal. I don't need it to be romantic love or have an expectation that I will grow old with the person. Nor do I need to be the only woman in my lover's life. I did find that it is important to me that the man be enchanted and enthralled with me. I want him to be considerably more excited about *having sex with me* than about *having sex*.

### Almost "there"...
I tried leaving out this component with a perfectly lovely man. He was an exceptional dancer and someone I'd known in college and reconnected with years later. He had many attributes I enjoyed—skilled dancer, good kisser, black-belt martial artist. He was also a person

whom I liked and respected, and with whom I felt safe. He was clear in communication, gracious in making time for me, and a charmingly attentive lover. I never had to guess where I stood, and always felt like a priority. He had great regard for me as a person, and we stayed in touch awhile after we stopped being lovers.

So, what, you may be wondering, was the downside? Well, while he was certainly sexually attracted to me, my body type was not his most preferred. He liked me very well, but he didn't adore me. Even though I enjoyed my time in his bed, I also quickly discovered it wasn't kind to me to put myself there.

I struggle to accept the fact that my body is larger and curvier than is generally approved of by society and the media. I have had many lovers who adore my body, who find it breathtaking and lovely. It is kinder to me to select my lovers from among those who are truly taken with my physical body as well as my mind and spirit. I do best with those who adore me, rather than simply think I am a delightful person with whom to scratch a mutual itch. I like sexual attention that is focused and very, very personal.

## Even closer...

One of the men I spent time with was a young Marine, a sweet boy, several years younger than I. I played as much the role of cheerleader or mentor as lover with him. I coached him in being direct about his goals and inviting women to play rather than saying he was looking for true love in order to woo women to his bed for a one night stand. While he was less mature and less giving than my aforementioned martial artist, he proved more deeply satisfying because he thought I was beautiful, wise, and wonderful, and said so often. At the point he cancelled plans with me, and then sent me a picture of himself out with another woman as part of a distribution list, I knew that my time with him had come to an end. But I enjoyed him thoroughly and did not begrudge his wandering attention.

## A cosmic curveball…

I did have one experience of being swept away by a passionate and poetic declaration of feeling that proved disappointing. I will say here that not every man looks at me. In fact, I'm tempted to say that most do not. But the ones who do are often deeply struck by me. So, having a man declare in impassioned terms that I am wondrous is not an entirely unusual experience.

The evening that this flowery fellow first tried to seduce me was charming. He whispered beautiful words in my ear, kissed me passionately and attempted to persuade me to share his bed. I was deeply tempted but insisted that I know him at least twenty-four hours before having sex with him. That was moving extremely fast for me. Still, we parted that night with an understanding that we would likely share a bed the following evening. He was handsome and charming and paid lovely attention to me through the next day.

Yet, by evening he was tired and less poetic. There was a woman with him and I kept getting the vibe that they were involved, despite his insistence that they were just friends. It was a good lesson in listening to my intuition. I make it a personal policy to make sure the women around me are having fun before the men. It just seems to work better that way, and it results in lots of women who are delighted to let me flirt with and kiss their husbands. In this case, this other woman was listening to her lover deny their sexual relationship in his quest for his next seduction. While she went along with it, and she and I later became dear friends, it made for an uncomfortable energy as he kept her around just long enough to see if he could get us both into bed together.

The experience was disappointing. For all the beautiful words and passionate promises, he seemed to assume that he had done his part of the work by getting me into bed. He's the only man who ever argued with me about using a condom. What I regret is that I didn't honor myself enough to say, "No, I changed my mind, this isn't feeling good." In some ways I still had a good time. I like sex and it's pretty easy to find enjoyment. Yet, the energy afterwards left me feeling icky. He didn't even take the time to stop by and say good-bye the next morning before he left. I was sort of bemused by the experience. I simply hadn't ever had someone who shared my bed treat me as less than a friend.

I ended up writing to him to connect, just because it felt painful to leave the encounter on such unsatisfying terms. He wrote me long emails filled with lovely poetry. For reasons I can't begin to explain, I felt the need to repeat the experience. I suppose I just couldn't believe it had been that bad, given that it had that great of an advertisement. So, I got the real scoop on the woman who lived with him, explained that condoms would be used, no arguments, and planned to spend time with him the first night of a camping event, when he would be less tired.

The second time was even worse. By the time he left around dawn, I knew that no matter how prettily he spoke, this was not someone I wanted in my bed. He was all about me pleasing him, and my other lovers, before and after, have all looked to my pleasure before their own. There was no tenderness of touch or holding once the sex was complete. Touch was about getting more sex, not connecting. And, he sulked when I declined another round of sex around dawn.

His passionate emails prior to the event had spoken of wanting to spend the entire weekend with me. I had been evasive; remembering the last time, I wasn't sure I wanted to arrange for more than one night with him. Well, as it turned out, he invited another woman to meet him there. Rather than explaining that he had other plans, he simply assured her that I was "just a friend" without ever letting me know she was coming. I was annoyed on so many levels. I wouldn't have minded him having another date, but not to tell me directly and to talk to me about spending a full weekend together while making other plans annoyed me. Of course, while the universe is seldom fair, it is just. This new lady of his had much too much to drink, kissed all the other men in camp, and then threw up on him. Sadly, I missed it, but I was otherwise occupied that night.

In fairness to him, I don't believe it was simply about saying whatever it took to get me into bed. I believe this man was really caught up in his own image and idea of himself as this romantic, poetic seducer and lover of women. He believed his own "Don Juan" story.

## …And then a healing

The universe always seems to take good care of me. I came away from this encounter feeling painful about the whole thing. It felt icky that I had allowed this man to touch me. I'd gotten the answer that I needed, that the lovely words didn't translate into true honoring of me or my body. The next day I met a man who had been my lover about a year before. He was someone who had simply stopped dead in his tracks at the sight of me. He was delighted to see me again.

The night found him in my tent. I was so grateful to him because every word, every touch, every bit of his energy was about honoring me and my body. He was skillful, experienced, and knew exactly how to please a woman. It wasn't about getting laid, but about getting to spend time with me. He made love to me slowly, saying he wasn't in a hurry. He touched me, aroused me, and worshipped me. It washed away the pain and distaste of the night before. I was deeply grateful for that time. His healing attention anchored in my body the feeling of being adored, honored, and pleasured. I don't think he understood my gratitude, for he simply seemed to think that his lovemaking was only what I was due.

All of this experience can be distilled down into a couple of quick tests for choosing lovers:

## Test # 1

First of all, who comes first? Not literally, although that's important, too. What I mean is please consider where the man (or woman) you are considering taking to your bed would rate your pleasure.

**If your potential lover is more interested** in you having a good experience, emotionally and physically, than he is in his own gratification, this has a good chance of leading to a more than satisfactory experience. Believe me when I say that such men are in plentiful supply. They aren't always the most handsome or the most confident, yet in their hearts they worship and honor women.

**If the person is equally invested in your** pleasure as in his own, this can be a pleasant evening. I personally like the idea that nice guys finish last—spending their energy to gratify their partner before thinking of what they want—but if you feel drawn, this can still be a nice experience.

**However, if you meet someone who is clearly more interested** in getting what he wants than attending to your emotional well-being or physical gratification, I recommend walking away. No matter how charming, seductive, poetic, and nice he may be in his quest for what he wants, that charm is conditional. The minute this person has what he wants or isn't getting his, the pleasantness of the experience quickly diminishes. For me, opening myself up to create powerful sexual intimacy leaves me too vulnerable energetically and physically to risk with someone who doesn't have my best interests at heart.

**More extremely good reasons to say no:** If a man ever sulks, blames, calls names, or otherwise tries to emotionally manipulate or punish a woman for not having sex, he's putting her emotional well-being below his desire for his own gratification. If he complains about being left with an erection, fails to take a no with grace and respect, or withdraws affection when sex doesn't happen when he wants it, it is not kind to yourself to spend time in his bed. There are far too many men out there who would never dream of engaging in such antics to waste time with those who would, and trust me, you deserve better.

So, ask yourself before taking a lover where he puts your pleasure–above, equal to or below his own. If it's above, go for it. If equal, it's a judgment call. If it's below, back away. I've just had way better experiences with those who want my pleasure more than they want their own, and profound pleasure is had by all in those situations.

# Test # 2

The second recommended test is making sure the following statement holds true to say of yourself and your potential lover: "I like myself when I'm with you. You bring out the best in me." Without going into stories of good, bad, right or wrong, just take note of how that person makes you feel. If you feel strong, confident, happy, good, that's great. My martial artist passed the "more concerned with my pleasure than his own" test, but failed this one. Not that he was bad, but I didn't like the way I felt with the insecurity that being with him brought up. My less attentive, less sexually skillful Marine was better because I did like myself with him; he brought out some of my best qualities.

## Finding what fits

One of the most valuable things about having taken my journey of sexual exploration and gained some experience is being able to know what fits for me and what doesn't, without having to try it on. As I mentioned, along the way, I identified that one of the most important things for me with a lover is feeling adored. I need to feel cherished, valued, and important.

One such friend of mine breaks more dates with me than he keeps. It's just his nature to struggle with schedule. Despite this, I still make time for him because his deep adoration, admiration, and enjoyment of being with me shine out of his heart every second we're together. I don't enjoy the unreliability of making plans with him. But when I spend time with him, my heart gets filled up so quickly that it's totally worth the inconvenience. I like myself when I'm with him.

In contrast, I found myself pulling away from a connection to a nice, handsome, successful, and articulate businessman. He was just the kind of man your mother would want you to bring home (if I had that kind of mother, which, happily, I don't). Unfortunately, he wasn't making the kind of heart connection I needed. I felt that he liked me, enjoyed my company, and respected me—but didn't adore me. Further, I found that with him my insecurities got stirred up. I felt vulnerable and as if he just wasn't that into me, even though it was clear he liked me. Whether that was true or not, the feeling made me enjoy the time with him less. I played around sexually with him, and was startled to find my usual passionate, intense, response didn't happen, despite his skillful participation. I just wasn't feeling safe enough to fully open myself up to sexual intimacy with him and run energy at the level of intensity that makes sex a powerful, compelling, healing experience for both partners.

Another experience that came up in the last year was making a great connection with someone and finding that he was just too busy to make much time for me. I had been wrestling with that issue recently and painfully in another relationship. I found that I wasn't able to not take it personally, and I was adamant that I didn't want to spend my energy chasing someone or trying to get his attention. The bottom line was that I wasn't a high priority compared to the other things going on in his life, however much he liked me. His actions made that clear. So, I chose to step away, even though I felt a bit sad about it. Another time I would have struggled, tried to get more of his time and attention, beaten up on myself for not being more understanding, and generally wasted a lot of energy. It felt kinder and more self-respecting to simply note that I wasn't getting what I needed emotionally, and step away.

I remember sitting with a group of friends while one of the men was pontificating about the difference between a "lady" and a "slut." A lady could have all the sex she wanted, he claimed, but she had feelings for the men she slept with. A slut, on the other hand, had sex without love. I responded that I felt like it would be good for women to have the space and the option of having sex, just for the pure, unmitigated experience of sex—to learn about themselves, their bodies, to enjoy pleasure, whatever, just sex as an end in and of itself. I went on to comment that surely women should have access to sexuality as free, consenting adults without being condemned as "bad" if they didn't love their partners.

I remain bothered by this idea that if a woman chooses to enjoy sex for the sake of sex, that's somehow bad or wrong. I have felt a measure of envy for the women I know who can play with sex more casually.

## The love hormone

In navigating the emotional side of sexuality, it's useful to understand that sex, especially good sex with lots of foreplay, will release oxytocin, the bonding hormone. It can make you feel in love. After all, it's designed to get women to feed and cuddle their babies at 3 a.m., instead of hating them when they start screaming for the fifth night in a row.

It's good to understand how intensely you are affected by this hormone, since it's different for everyone. Feeling in love with your life partner after sex is a grand thing. However, falling into bed casually with someone who isn't suited to be part of a relationship, and finding yourself in love with them the next day can be inconvenient. Both men and women release oxytocin, so either partner can start casually and get carried away by hormone-induced love.

Human beings tend to judge another's thoughts and reactions against their own. So, if you're a woman who tends to develop feelings for lovers when the sex is really good, it's easy to assume that men will have the same experience. I've seen that men can be very focused on getting sex, but that focus can shift to something else immediately following sex, and it's not necessarily love! For me, the personal rule of needing to know someone and spend a bit of time with them before becoming sexual has served me well, because I am hurt if the post-sexual emotional connection is colder on his side than it was before we ended up in bed.

What I learned about myself is that I don't need a committed relationship to make a sexual relationship work. A good, solid friendship will do just fine. But anything less than the emotional warmth of friendship is too casual a connection to go with sexuality. I do "friends with benefits" well. One night stands don't work for me; the emotional overhead is too high. In opening myself to a new partner, there's too much energy that goes into the experience for it to feel worthwhile to me if it's a one-time thing.

# Chapter 4—Attraction

I have often heard a lament in the dating game, regarding attraction. It seems to fall into one of three categories. Either the woman is complaining about being attracted to the wrong sort of men, or that she is attracting the wrong sort of men, or that no men are attracted to her at all.

## Who we attract or feel attraction for…

Part of what plays out in the attraction game is what's really going on at a deep level. The more healed we are, the more work we've done on ourselves, the more available we are to see other people as they truly are. As we heal, we see others less as mirrors for whatever we're working on and we're also less inclined to project our fantasies on to them.

Often when it comes to relationships, there's a level of ambivalence; one aspect of our being wants a partner more than anything, yet another part wants nothing to do with another relationship. A relationship offers intimacy, sex, companionship, and many other wonderful things that we long for—but relationships also stir up our deepest wounds and make us feel most vulnerable. The same unhealed part (which I believe everyone has to some degree) that longs for the love of another to make up for incomplete self-love, also fears the vulnerability and potential for loss and rejection in a relationship.

When potential partners look at you, the healthier they are, the more accurately they will be able to read your true availability for a relationship. One of my clients had a deep connection with her father, and when he died, she continued with a lot of her energy and attention tied up in missing him and holding onto his energy. So, to someone reading her energy as it was, rather than projecting, it would have felt like she was already in a relationship. The man who felt this couldn't have told you why, probably, but he just instinctively knew that she wasn't really receptive and moved on.

Similarly, if a woman is more in a place of wishing to be over her last partner than actually healed from the wounds of her last relationship, a person who is meeting her (without projecting a fantasy) will simply get the sense that she's not really available or interested. However, if the person meeting her has an unhealed wound themselves from a partner who wasn't truly available to them, that person might in turn be drawn to her, sensing a situation that allows them to engage with the unhealed wound. This speaks to the subtle, energetic aspects of attraction as it interacts with each person's level of insight and self-knowledge.

## Wanting the wrong type of partner

As far as being attracted to what seems to be the wrong sort of partner, this is often a call for healing. If we had an emotionally absent father, or a father with a rage problem, we are seeking to heal those wounds. If our mother was emotionally distant, we may choose a partner with that same quality. By finding a partner who has the same issue, but professes a deep, passionate devotion to us, we can work with coming to a different outcome.

Perhaps we learn not to fear the rage, or we choose to emotionally disengage from that kind of person. There's a chance to deal with the same situation as an empowered adult, with all the options and choices we didn't have as children. We may experience suffering as adults with these partners, but our deeper purpose is to rewrite a story. We are instinctively compelled to try to heal our deepest wounds. A deep love is a powerful bribe to work through things that hurt rather than running away.

So why don't we pick the "right" partner? It's extremely uncomfortable to be in the company of someone who loves us and treats us better than we treat ourselves. And let's face it: the codependent, rescuing, over-giving type who is drawn to victims isn't a lot of fun. He or she may look better than the abusive jerk, but can and will actually sabotage a partner's movement toward growth and health—because once the partner's no longer a victim, the rescuer isn't needed any more. So, as we grow and heal, our preferred partners are people who are more mature and giving. And as we begin to become more whole, especially in the area of inner-child work, healthier and more loving partners become more attractive and interesting.

## When the wrong partner wants you

Sometimes it seems like a series of "Mr. or Mrs. Wrongs" are drawn to you. People who are not the least bit attractive to you may throw themselves in your path. I find the best way to deal with this is to simply acknowledge the compliment that someone is taken with me and let him or her know, as kindly as possible, that I'm not available. Whenever I'm shining in public in some way, it's not unusual for an unsuitable person to become uncomfortably focused on me. Having inappropriate people throw themselves at you doesn't mean there's something out of alignment in you; they may simply be responding to your light, seeking a healing opportunity, or projecting their own fantasies onto you.

## Not interested at all—"I don't feel sexy"

Women who have experienced sexual trauma can feel safest in the world if they don't feel sexually attractive. It's often not a conscious thing. I have worked with women who wanted very much to lose weight, only to notice on the shamanic level the part of them that desperately didn't want to lose weight. The more we feel a sense of vulnerability to violence, the more likely we are to try to protect ourselves by not being noticed by the predator. Women gain weight, wear drab clothes, avoid eye contact with strangers, and try not to call too much attention or notice. In the absence of a faith in their ability to spot a dangerous man, women treat all men like predators, potentially dangerous. Carrying extra weight, and even more so, the perception that no one would be attracted to you, is a powerful shield to tune out romantic or sexual attention.

Yet, the women who snap the most heads, who have men falling down at their feet, aren't, in my experience, the prettiest, thinnest women. It tends to be the women who just make eye contact with men and smile. Feeling attractive and good about yourself and being interested in connecting is tremendously attractive. This combination will draw people looking to connect, romantically and sexually.

When a woman is keeping score about how attracted men are to her, for it to be accurate, she needs to count all the men who try to talk to her, say hello, or catch her eye—not just the ones she happens to fixate on. It's also important to remember that men have learned to be cautious and feel out the territory before giving clear signals of attraction. No one likes rejection, and women can give confusing mixed signals, especially if they are most open with men they are not sexually attracted to.

One of the simpler reasons for not feeling attractive may be that you're just not seeing what's in front of your nose. Many women get shy and freeze up around men they are attracted to. When feeling shy, the natural response is to hide and try not to be seen, so these men don't notice them. These same women are often relaxed, open, and natural with men they're not attracted to. There's no pressure, so it's easy to just enjoy being with the other person. The result can be that you keep having guys you're not attracted to falling head over heels for you. Realize that this tells you that men find you incredibly attractive when they get to see your natural, open, relaxed energy.

It's also possible that you don't notice all the men who would gladly fall down at your feet with the least encouragement. I am firmly of the belief that when a woman is learning about her own sexual attractiveness, she needs spotters. It feels vulnerable to be caught staring, as a man or a woman. So, if someone is looking at you, they'll probably look away when you look over. For example, I went clubbing one night with a group of friends, wearing a leather corset that showed a good deal of cleavage. For the first few hours, before people were drinking, I swear I didn't see a single man look at me. However, my friends were able to report many craned necks and distracted head snaps. The oglers were all just looking away when I looked. Later in the evening, when the crowd became less sober and thereby less inhibited, I got plenty of obvious attention, and, as I recall, a few marriage proposals.

I've had a number of occasions watching some man fling himself at one of my friends and watching her assume he was just being friendly. I have had many conversations with friends who explained that the man at the party trying to make conversation with me was interested. Somehow the dumbfounded, enthralled look is totally obvious to an outside observer, but lost on the individual being admired. If a man or a woman doesn't think of themselves as attractive, getting them to notice that you disagree can be impossibly uphill work.

I'd spent a great deal of my life feeling invisible, boring, and out of place socially. I also felt too tall and generally unattractive. At one point a very attractive man spent the better part of an hour trying to talk me into walking over to a party with him. Six months later, years before my kissing quest, when he went out of his way to kiss me (and wow, let me say the man could kiss!) it dawned on me that he was interested. I simply didn't see myself as sexually attractive, so I had no clue he was interested.

In my kissing quest, I learned about the nature of sexual energy. I learned how to create and turn on a field around me, and to invite people to come and play in it. Not every man responds to it, but more often than not, when I'm in that mode, I turn heads and get asked out. In my experience, people respond to energy far more than looks.

# Chapter 5—Embracing What Is

Imagine the archetypal, essential feminine divine as a large sphere, containing all the light and dark, all the wonderful and terrible, and wonderfully terrible aspects of woman. She is comprised of the maiden, mother, and crone. She holds the energy of Kali at her most destructive, and includes Kuan Yin and Mother Mary. This sphere holds the archetypal energy of wife, mother, warrior, daughter, grandmother, hermit, magician, wise woman, queen, priestess, beggar, even madwoman.

Our modern culture takes that sphere and compresses it, distorts it, rejects pieces, and over-amplifies others. This misshapen lump is what our culture would have us believe represents the nature of women. Different areas of the sphere are charged with various projections. For example, the nice, kind, nurturing, thoughtful, caretaking aspects are highlighted, praised, and sometimes taken as the whole.

The cultural, family, and romantic relationship pressures to conform to this distortion of the feminine leads many women to develop an adversarial relationship with themselves, sorting aspects of the self into categories of "good" and "bad." Our self-esteem becomes dependent on how effectively we can disown certain aspects of ourselves. These aspects become what are generally referred to in the metaphysical community as our shadows. Our shadows, aspects of ourselves that are disowned and disenfranchised, include all the things about ourselves that we are ashamed of and wish would go away. They can be made up of many things: emotions that we have polarized as "bad," such as anger or sadness; traits and qualities that we have been made to feel ashamed of; or aspects of our sexuality.

## Living with our shadow

Our shadow is often what we judge most harshly in others. If we are enduring the pain of suppressing and disconnecting from some part of ourselves, it's hard to be gracious to people who are expressing and freely embodying that aspect. For example, if I tie myself in knots to keep my word about every commitment I make, I am likely to react negatively to someone who cancels an appointment because they find that it isn't right for them to keep it. If I am denying myself the flexibility of putting myself first and renegotiating commitments based on my current needs, I'm going to be very jealous and therefore judgmental of someone who takes care of themselves by changing plans, especially if they are happy and still seem to have the love and respect of those around them. When these disowned parts are something as primal and integral as our sexuality, the intensity of the pain, longing, and judgment that spring up around shadow are greatly increased.

Hollywood makes money by blending together multiple shadow aspects of the feminine. The resulting archetype is no less two-dimensional than the other stereotypes of women. However, by blending in a female character an intense, direct, passionate sexuality with dangerous warrior abilities, people can engage with their deep longing for expression of these parts in a safe way. This could be Lara Croft-Tomb Raider, Cat Woman, or any of Charlie's Angels.

For women, the chance to watch and therefore live vicariously for an hour or two as a passionate, sensual, sexy woman who knows exactly what she wants is delightful. In the magical Hollywood world, we can fantasize about being able to hurt and humiliate anyone who dared presume to punish us for being sexual. We can embrace and stimulate the warrior part, the part of ourselves that is willing to be as big and terrible and forceful as is needed. Anyone who has ever swallowed a "Get your hands the fuck off me!!!" and settled for simply pulling away gently or gritting her teeth, can likely find the part of her that longs to be able to throw the man across the room for touching her without permission. After all, if we could be deadly and dangerous enough, we could claim our sexuality without needing to fear male violence. Plus, that confident woman of the big screen seems to be immune to the unkind judgments of others.

Men resonate to this richness as well. Men adore movies with women who kick ass and take names. While some men are intimidated, many respond intensely to women who are in their power in an authentic way in the real world. It's not all men, of course. Some men still have a problem with women warrior types and reject them and seek women to date and marry who are not expressing that energy. Some men lost interest when I told them I was an engineer. Others backed away when I asked to be kissed. But a lot of them didn't and don't.

I've met men who have been excited that I hold an engineering degree. "She's smart and capable and spending time with me, yeah!" was often the reaction. There are many men who are weary and frustrated by women who are so good about conforming to the gender roles of society. What men seemed to like about the kissing quest (after the fact that they got to kiss me) was the chance to connect with a woman who was being clear about what she wanted, asking for it, then receiving it.

The more deeply you embrace the full territory, light and dark, of being a woman, the more comfortable it is to be in your own skin. This frees up more life for energy to spend however you wish. And, far from scaring all the men away with this authentic, non-society approved way of being in the world, you will attract a whole new group of men who adore women in their power. In my experience, these guys are much more worthwhile. If you're going to be embraced by some people and judged by others no matter what you do, it seems only logical to do what is going to make you the happiest overall. Allowing ourselves to be whole instead of merely pleasing creates a far more fulfilling life.

# The lessons of infidelity

One of my own deepest experiences of embracing shadow came with my Disappearing Man. The Disappearing Man reference comes from a glorious song by that name, written by Dave Carter and sung by Tracy Grammer. It speaks of the right of passage of taking a lover whom you ache for, who is the embodiment of the masculine divine. And it speaks of losing him, "So the night comes and goes…and he rides off gay and lawless as the morning that you met." It speaks of the pain of that loss, "Will you stand in the road, waiting for another searcher—will you weep soft and low, in the voice that your mother used to use?" and of the other side of that pain: finding the power and strength to stand alone and flourish, "bright and fierce."

This song summed up that part of my sexual journey. My Disappearing Man was married, but delighted to share my bed, provided I understood about his wife. My rule before then had been and remains, "No married men unless I have the wife's permission." As someone who takes ethics unbelievably seriously, crossing that line was the death of who I thought I was. Yet, this man was, for me, the embodiment of the masculine divine and a symbol of a sexual experience with a man who was confident, assured, and skillful. I longed for some time to be in his bed like I have seldom yearned for anything.

There's a part of me that, when I tell this story, instantly wants to explain and mitigate the statement of, "Yes, I had sex with a married man without his wife's permission." So I'm going to let her have her say. I was not his first lover outside his marriage, or his last, and I spent a tremendous amount of time assuring myself that the only person I was seriously at risk of hurting was myself. Luckily, I was correct in my risk assessment.

Yet, no stories of his loveless marriage or my care change the fact that I crossed a line in my personal code of ethics. As much as there is a part of me that wants to explain or justify, there's a knowing that there is no explanation or justification. It was simply a choice. I wanted the experience enough to sacrifice an idea of who I thought I was, an idea I was pretty invested in. It meant giving up an idea of myself as better than people who cheat on partners and a level of ethical superiority. When I made the choice, I mourned the loss of this idea of myself as ethically perfect, as someone who would never cross a line, no matter the temptation.

And, on the other side of this experience, I found I liked Katie who chose to sleep with a married man better than Katie who would never sleep with a married man. It made me more compassionate and gave me deeper insight. I can understand and find within myself what it is to desire someone or something so strongly that other things don't matter. Even when this man, as the song describes, wandered away, distracted, almost as soon as we had begun, I didn't regret the experience. I don't regret it now, for all the reasons I've given—and the memory of the pain is part of the overall experience.

## Embracing the past

As part of my soul retrieval process, I ask clients to share anything (that they are comfortable sharing) about their past and current situation that may relate to soul loss. I often hear clients tell me how bad they were in the past. It makes me sad how many women who are now choosing monogamy talk about being more sexual as though it was a self-destructive behavior that they have gotten over.

"I went through this phase where I was very promiscuous and had a lot of lovers, so I'm sure I lost some parts there. It was bad, but now I'm with my husband/boyfriend." It's regrettable that a woman's sexual exploration is so often described as bad or shallow or a sign of low self-esteem instead of a beautiful, sacred journey to self-knowledge.

For a woman who spends some time exploring her sexuality, having casual lovers, and then finds a monogamous relationship that makes her happy, all of this is a great journey. Sexual experience can lead to a solid self-knowledge making the things one gives up for monogamy (like having lovers and the excitement of the unknown) totally worth the security and intimacy of an exclusive relationship.

Perhaps one day she finds herself yearning for the days when she was single and having sex with many partners. Many people label themselves as bad for feeling this way, shaming themselves, and attempting to suppress these feelings. What if instead this longing was simply taken as a reminder that she found a way to get her needs met in the past, and can find an appropriate way to get her needs met now — as if looking outside, reading the temperature, and putting on an extra layer if it's cold? Most people don't judge the weather if it's 40 degrees outside; they just dress accordingly.

Instead of beating up on herself, now this woman can play detective and investigate the cause of these feelings. Is she missing being the center of attention? Perhaps she would do well to go out dancing with her friends or join a theatre group. Is she missing feeling admired and special and being courted? Perhaps it's time for her and her partner to have date nights. Maybe deeper healing in the relationship is needed. When these feelings are ignored, we can develop a deep well of pain and unmet needs, because instead of responding to the indicators that something isn't working, we beat ourselves up for having them. This unwillingness to look at what our feelings and hearts are telling us is part of what sets the stage for breaking promises of monogamy.

When working with finding and exploring our shadow part, it's helpful to look at the areas of the hottest buttons and the largest triggers. When we find the areas that bring about the strongest, knee-jerk judgments, there is a great healing opportunity. I find the area of sexual fidelity extremely rich learning ground for exploring shadow. Many people have huge, angry judgments about those who cheat on their partners. If we can come to terms with understanding this from a more compassionate perspective than simply wrong and bad, we deepen our ability for self-love about the "wrong" choices we might make even if we're not engaged in affairs in any way.

One client came to me and told me she was having an affair. She told me about how she had no intention of getting involved, hadn't believed herself even capable of sexual passion at her age, and found herself swept away by it. When I talked to her guides, they were delighted and happy for her, no judgment; in fact they were celebrating. She was coming back to life, opening and awakening a deep part of herself. Part of her journey towards health and wholeness required her to step away from her very safe but emotionally absent husband. Her husband wasn't a bad guy, but he was bad for her. It was a tough road, and both people grew a lot and became happier in their lives when the marriage ended.

Another client came to me and talked about how her husband had cheated on her. She was deeply in love with another man, but hadn't acted on it physically. She was very indignant at her husband's behavior. Yet, she had been deeply unhappy in her marriage before the affair, and some part of her was hoping her husband would leave her. The guides wanted to know what it would take for her to walk away from a situation that was miserable for her. Her controlling, emotionally abusive husband had blamed her for changing and said the affair was her fault; that she was pushing him away. I realized what she needed to hear wasn't, "No, it's not your fault", but rather "If you are pushing him away, congratulations, you're taking really good care of yourself. That's a smart move, given what you really want."

A third client talked to me about her remorse and shame at having had some relationships with married men. Her father had left when she was young. The guides showed me that energetically, when her father left for another woman, he hadn't kept good boundaries about the difference between his daughter and his wife, lumping them both together in his bitter feelings about women in general. The guides said that the time she spent with married men was part of her healing process. One of the gifts is that if a man is married and having a sexual relationship on the side, he is often jumping through hoops to keep the other woman happy. It allowed my client to be in the role of the important woman that she was denied with her father. Once she had that experience, she was able to heal and no longer felt interested in spending time with married men.

Human beings promise to forsake all others and then break their word. It's been done throughout the ages. As a shamanic practitioner, I have a unique understanding of the gifts and needs that get met when someone breaks a marriage vow. As a healing practitioner, I also have a keen sense of the pain, shame, guilt, and agony that can be created by these choices, whichever role one plays in the drama.

## A new perspective

Wouldn't it be interesting if the now sober alcoholic told this story:

> I had all this pain and emotion that I didn't know how to deal with. I am grateful to the alcohol because I think I would have killed myself if I didn't have a way to numb the pain. I honor the time I spent drinking because it allowed me to survive and begin to learn other tools.
>
> Then Alcoholics Anonymous gave me better tools and taught me how to get through the pain. I connected with other people who had the same experiences and could follow their example for dealing with pain while sober. Once I had those tools, even though it was hard, I gave up the alcohol because it was numbing the pain at the cost of sabotaging anything that would make me happy—my job, my relationships, my health. I honor what alcohol did for me, and I'm grateful that I don't need it anymore, because the price for what it gave me was very high. I don't drink anymore because drinking is not kind to me.

I love this because there's no judgment, just a deep honoring of the self and of the choices of the past, the present, and the journey in-between. My understanding of how AA and the Twelve Step® programs work is that in fact the Steps help sober alcoholics find freedom from a past of self-hatred and a deeper understanding of the importance of a spiritual life in staying sober. In contrast, society telling the story that that the alcoholic is weak, bad, self-destructive, and wrong doesn't seem all that helpful to someone seeking the strength to make a change.

There's a painful disconnect within us when we make ourselves bad and wrong for who we were and what we did in the past. The complicated business of being human means we all have strategies, things we do, and ways of being in the world that strive to get our needs met. At the point that something stops working and is causing more pain than joy, hopefully we have the clarity, courage, and resources to change it at the right time for ourselves. What allowed us to survive as children was good, but we can come up with better strategies as adults when we have more choices.

But what about the men and women who cheat and don't care? I don't know, since I haven't met them. However, if the knowledge of the pain they'll inflict on the person they're married to isn't enough to deter them, other people going, "Shame, shame, you're bad" seems unlikely to discourage them.

In my own life, spending time with a dear friend who loved me deeply helped me step away from a relationship that was painful, unfulfilling, and dysfunctional. While I didn't have sex with the friend, nor cross lines in the physical world, the connection included the energy of passion and romantic love. The experience held up a mirror that showed me how starved I was for that type of loving energy, affection, and kindness. That experience didn't lead me to cheat, but it did provide impetus to leave a relationship that was not serving me—one of my more life-affirming choices, in retrospect. That experience, combined with my Disappearing Man, allows me to find in myself what I witness in those who are having affairs.

From a shamanic perspective, I understand that sometimes this cheating is an outward manifestation of a deeper imbalance in the individual or in a given relationship. Just as we begin to understand that certain emotional patterns may increase a genetic or environmental potential for some types of cancer, other energetic imbalances increase the potential for infidelity. Mostly we don't say cancer is bad or wrong, it just is. When humans experience cancer, there is pain and suffering and transformation. I've known people who embraced the gift of how cancer transformed their lives, as well as people who have died. Likewise, I know people who have embraced the gifts of their own affair, or their partners', and used the impetus for change that moved their life to a happier level.

When we embrace all of who we are, the light and the dark, we empower ourselves to see our partners clearly. We can see what is, rather than what we want this person to be. We create suffering when we argue with reality, wanting what is to be different. So, when a woman who has embraced her shadow comes across a potential partner who has cheated in the past and who is breathtakingly charming, she may choose to pass him up if she knows that she needs monogamy to feel safe and good in a relationship.

## Honoring what is

I certainly qualify as a woman who has ignored reality due to her desire for a fantasy about someone. In fact, it's been quite recently that I've wandered the paths of, "But our relationship will be different from all the others he's had because it's *me*," or used the excuse, "But he says he loves me more than anyone," as a reason to ignore what a man's actions were telling me. I have yet to meet the woman who has been in relationships who hasn't explored some of that territory with partners.

Often in hindsight we can see the signals that reality gave us that we ignored in favor of what we wanted to be true. When we argue with reality, or blame the other person, we make ourselves a victim and give up our power. In the interest of embracing all of ourselves, even the victim part, it's good to understand the payoff of being the victim. People will be on our side, indignant on our behalf. Our bad behavior and mistreatment of the other person can be excused or erased if we are the victim. Perhaps we can make the other person pay in some way. So, if someone is living as their victim self, the compassionate view is that they're taking care of themselves the best way they know how.

While I understand the payoffs and gifts of being in the victim role, and have spent time there myself, I also know that when I do that, I give up my power. If I'm the victim, someone else has power over my well-being and happiness, and that power is being used to create more suffering. Owning my poor choices, as painful as that may be, rejects blaming the other person for my unhappiness, and takes back my own control over my happiness. At the end of the day, not judging others isn't something I do for their sake; I do it for the sake of my own happiness, well-being, and self-love.

More often than people hanging on to roles as victims, I see people being too hard on themselves. Many of my clients are great at taking responsibility for their situations and the choices that got them there. But then they judge, criticize, and condemn themselves for being weak, needy, or stupid. You wouldn't look at your arm, see that you have a bleeding cut, and slap the cut for being a wound. But, when it comes to our emotional, interpersonal wounds, somehow we tend to whap them instead of applying first aid and rehab.

Please don't argue with reality about yourself. You are where you are. Don't think of yourself as bad for your wounds and choices. You've made the best choices to meet your needs based on the skills you had at the time, whether you picked a cheating or abusive partner, cheated on your partner, or none of the above. When you're ready, you'll make new choices that will meet your needs more fully. In holding compassion for people who make choices that cause pain to themselves and those around them, we learn to hold compassion for ourselves.

## Chapter 6—Sexual Healing

I am a shamanic practitioner who was molested as a child, so I have seen from the inside and outside how childhood molestation impacts sexuality and life in general. My history has given me a compassionate perspective from which to work with a number of clients with similar trauma.

A common result of molestation is that the victim's lower chakras[1] shut down. The root and the sacral chakras no longer allow energy to flow as it should through the body. If energy isn't running through these areas, the pain and damage isn't felt by the child. You might call it a form of dissociation; a common way for a child to deal with such overwhelming damage.

The root chakra contains the energy of joy, natural pleasure, passion, and connection to the earth. It is the chakra that draws down spiritual energy and causes it to assume a physical existence. The root chakra is the base from which the psychic channels emerge, and is related to physical processes of sexual intercourse, reproduction, and excretion, and the emotions, including fear and guilt, associated with them.

---

[1] The body has spinning energy centers that energetically look like spinning wheels and are called chakras (pronounced chuhkruhs), meaning *wheel* in Sanskrit. The seven main chakras are described as being aligned in an ascending column from the base of the spine to the top of the head. The root and the sacral chakras are located at the perineum and at the end of the spine, respectively.

The sacral chakra is related to sexuality, creativity, and emotion. This chakra is said to correspond to the endocrine system that produces the various sex hormones involved in the reproductive cycle, which may cause dramatic mood swings in both men and women. The potential for new growth, healthy creativity, and the direct expression of emotion is located here.

This works fairly well up until the victim begins to experience the changing hormones of adolescence and the subsequent awakening of their sexual being. I've found personally that I can be very sexual as long as the encounter is more about excitement than intimacy. If my partner is someone new, or hits some of my big turn-ons, the excitement and arousal can carry me through into a very enjoyable, exciting sexual experience.

The challenge happens when sex begins to encompass the territory of intimacy and love beyond excitement and intensity. Under these circumstances, when I'm with a partner I'm deeply connected to, I find that I can become reconnected to the painful past. All sorts of painful wounding gets stirred up, which can be overwhelming in its intensity. I have dealt with that (with someone I trust) by going into it, to have them hold me while I breathe through the emotions. I heal when I stay present with my partner and allow the emotions to rise and fall and flow through. This is terrifyingly intimate and vulnerable, especially for someone who was abused in their vulnerability as a child.

I tried other solutions first. Does this sound familiar? I tend to want sex less often with someone after the first few months of the relationship. In each case, I can look at that time when the sex becomes less frequent as also being a time when my issues start to creep into the experience. There may be subtle ways I'm not feeling safe, loved, or honored in the relationship.

## The truth of sex
Sex is a great truth-teller for me. If I'm not feeling warm, intimate, and connected to my partner on the deepest levels, I can ignore it outside the sexual experience. But running sexual energy into the lower chakras

also runs energy into areas where I'm holding onto feelings that are not being addressed. So, avoiding sex is one of the easiest ways to keep the waters smooth with someone I'm choosing to be with, while experiencing some underlying issues. Except, of course, my partner becomes unhappy about the absence of this aspect of our relationship, and then the lack of sex becomes an issue between us, highlighting that not all is well.

The other less than perfect solution is simply to dissociate to some degree or another. With my first lover, I hated the beginning of sex because that was when my wounds got the most triggered. If I could tune out and wait out that first part and get turned on enough, I could bypass the pain and have a very good time. It was only this horrible in-between time when the arousal of my body wasn't enough to overwhelm the awakening of all the other painful emotions that I found myself dreading.

As I mentioned before, I found later that my new lovers, people I wasn't truly intimate with—but very sexually excited by—always made for enjoyable experiences. As I grew into more intimate relationships, it was hard on my more serious lovers to see me being hugely flirtatious and passionate in the beginning, only to hide that part of myself away as we grew closer together as partners.

It seems to me that many women eventually become non-sexual in relationships. It's frequently just easier to focus on other aspects of our lives than to do the hard work of building trust and working through healing with a partner. Yet, as healing takes place, as sexuality is opened and expressed, the quality and delight of the experience is dramatically increased. For many who have decided to not express sexuality rather than work through these wounds, they haven't experienced the full ride, so they don't actually know what they're missing.

## Sex teaches one to be present
Being present with yourself through the sexual experience, going into the feelings, riding them through, finding the pleasure on the other

side, isn't just about sexual pleasure and intimacy with partners. This is a primal way to access intimacy with yourself. If you struggle with boundaries in your life, learning to be present with what you feel in bed can teach you to be present with what you feel in life. When we have poor boundaries, often it relates to not being present enough or feeling strong enough in the moment to notice and respond.

When something doesn't feel good, I've noticed a tendency in myself and a number of other women to be a bit disconnected. Part of it is our socialization to be nice; we're trained not to make a fuss and to please others. When there has been sexual trauma of some kind, the reaction that tells us something doesn't feel good is often hugely disproportional to the incident. For example, someone I find icky may touch my arm, and suddenly my body goes into full "flight or fight" mode. So, I end up spending all my energy and attention trying to suppress the excessive overreaction in the interest of appearing normal. Survivors of molestation are especially adept at appearing normal when things are terrible inside, but I know a lot of women without that trauma who have also mastered that skill.

I've had plenty of times when I've noted a knot in my stomach that I've been ignoring for a while. I try to make it go away, to suppress it. When that doesn't work, I begin tracking it back to the origin—and that's a skill greatly enhanced through shamanic practice! Often, whatever has triggered the response has happened quite a bit earlier. In being present and noticing the feelings are from the past, I empower myself to address those feelings now and make my life better.

As we heal from sexual trauma or just come into our power, there's a chance to move closer and closer to being able to react to a boundary being crossed in a way that is authentic and in the moment. How many times have you walked away mad at yourself for not saying something when someone crossed a line or made a hurtful comment? How often have you found yourself fuming to a friend days later about something that happened that you allowed in the moment? Instead of being available to say in the moment to the other person, "That doesn't feel good, stop," it's easy to get caught up in struggling with ourselves over our reaction.

## Listening to our own wisdom

As we heal and release old pain, we can hear ourselves clearly. The way I see it is that we have this part of ourselves, an inner voice that tells us as soon as something doesn't feel good. I think of this as my inner child because she simply reports back on how good or bad something feels without filtering her report through any story about it. Think about a baby. When the baby gets a shot, he or she likely begins to scream and cry. It hurt, it felt bad. When mom holds and cuddles the baby, the crying stops; that feels good and comforting. The baby doesn't suppress the crying because it hasn't been conditioned yet to believe it's bad to make a fuss, or that this person who's hurting you has good intentions.

As we get older, we begin to suppress feelings. Something happens that doesn't feel good and we stuff it down. We'll be made fun of on the playground if we cry, so we learn to hold back the tears. Our lower chakras are the perfect storage area or container for this kind of unprocessed emotional goop. To avoid the "goop" we put a powerful lid on the container. Every time a wound happens that we can't process in the moment, it gets stuffed into this container. So, the lid is under more and more pressure.

Over time, we spend more and more of our attention and energy holding that lid on. Perhaps we have things that relieve the pressure such as exercise, therapy, letting ourselves fall apart and cry from time to time. That flat tire can be a great chance to burst into tears and let some of the pressure out. It may feel awful at the time, but the next day tends to be much better.

The problem with pent up feelings is that some amount of our energy is constantly engaged with holding them down. As long as that's the case, the inner voice of truth that says someone has crossed our boundary, someone isn't safe for us, or a situation is bad news, will be suppressed and stuffed down. The same voice of our intuition that tells us how we feel about what's happening in the moment has also been trying to tell us about the suppressed feelings. Ignoring that voice can become an incredibly well developed, if not so helpful, skill.

## Emotional pressure cooker

In other words, we can't simultaneously be holding a lid on our unprocessed emotions and have space for an emotional signal to arise that something feels bad. There's too much of a risk that the emotional gunk could come exploding forth at an inopportune moment. So, when we first get the signal, it pushes at the lid of our suppressed emotions, and we automatically press that lid down harder. If the pain of the experience is big enough or stirs up something that has a big emotional charge, the lid may get blasted off. Then we might scream or rant or cry and feel embarrassed by the disproportional emotional response. So, instead of being able to react appropriately to the situation our emotions are signaling as a problem, we're fully engaged with the external crisis of trying not to fall apart.

We often learn to suppress our emotions at all costs while growing up. It could be our peers, our parents or someone else who punishes or shames us for being emotional. Perhaps someone else gets really triggered and hurt by our feelings and we feel responsible. Boys, even more than girls, get punished and shamed for vulnerable feelings. As adult women, we often look to our male partners—who have been socialized to not acknowledge their own feelings—to support us in our emotions. Not only is there a lack of skill, but as discussed in regards to shadow, it's hard to be tolerant of someone who is expressing a part of the human experience that you are actively denying yourself. So, the expected reaction that a male partner will treat a woman's emotions as weak, illogical, or self-indulgent may be another reason for denying and suppressing them.

As adults, it may take a good bit of conscious work to rewrite our early training about emotions and find a new way of being that allows and honors what we're feeling. We can begin by choosing the people in our lives and learning self-nurturing skills. As we delve into self-healing, we empty out that container of festering, suppressed emotion. We learn to release and process our emotions as they arise, and suddenly our life force energy is no longer depleted with all the energy it takes to shut down old and new feelings. When we keep that inner container and the area of our lower chakras flushed and cleared with energy flowing through, we enjoy both vitality and peace. Plus, we get the signal when our boundaries are crossed and something doesn't feel good, in the moment.

Over time, we can unlearn our old responses, and the lag time between the moment when we consciously notice something doesn't feel good and the moment we respond becomes shorter and shorter. We get practiced with saying "no" with grace and ease and, surprisingly, people don't take offense.

## Kindness heals

When we are kind to ourselves, accepting and loving of ourselves, we find that someone else's disapproval, while it may never be a fun experience, isn't devastating. We stop needing to manipulate and control in order to be safe. While those were prime survival strategies as a child, they don't serve nearly so well in our adult lives.

Imagine if you will what it would be like to completely release trying to make people like you or please them. Imagine if you only did what felt authentically good to you. You go to work because it feels better to get the paycheck than deal with what it would be like not to have one. You don't attend that baby shower because it doesn't sound fun and you don't feel close enough to the person to feel a stronger desire to witness and be part of that moment in their lives. You stop doing and pleasing others in a hundred ways. Out of that hundred choices not to please, someone is upset with you for two of them.

However, you have saved such a vast amount of energy and been so kind to yourself, that the two moments of people being upset are easily processed, and you have a tremendous amount of energy left over. There are many ways that you've just been in the moment, having a good time, instead of worrying about other people being happy or pleased with you. This allows your personal energy to be much higher, more vibrant. You're having fun and people love being with you.

Suddenly, you're getting more approval, attention, and praise from those around you as a result of not pleasing. Can you imagine what you could do with all that spare energy?

My personal journey down that path continues to enrich the ways I see and relate to myself and others. The less I please, the less I worry about what people will think, the less I edit, the more people like me. People are drawn to my energy, they have a strong positive response to me——they want my attention! When I was people-pleasing and trying to be liked, I got less positive regard, because people couldn't connect with the real me. However good a job I did of giving them things they liked, it felt disingenuous on some level. The people I attracted in pleasing mode were ones who were available for the other half of a codependent engagement where I would care-take. Their dependence on me was a way of getting my attention needs met, allowing me to feel important and special.

## The pain of healing

In regards to boundaries, one of the things I talk to my clients (and myself) about is being patient with the process. The people who say "no" with grace and ease and love either have an amazing natural talent or a lot of practice. We seem to expect that after a lifetime of pleasing others and suppressing our boundaries, we are a failure if we don't achieve that level of grace when we start. It's kind of like expecting a baby to get up for the first time and walk with ease and balance, no falling down, no learning curve. Another part of the process to consider is that when one embarks on a journey of healing sexuality (or healing in general), there may be a time when things seem to hurt more than they did before the healing happened.

In the face of too much pain or trauma to process, we seek to protect the essence of our being through soul loss or dissociation, in which we send part of our energy away from the situation. In addition, we shut down parts of our being. This numbness can help us to survive, function, and deal with things. Much like a tourniquet placed on a leg or an arm that is bleeding from an open artery, we preserve ourselves by shutting down in the face of pain, trauma, and damage that we don't have the resources to heal.

This energetic tourniquet cuts off the life force energy to certain parts of our being. Just as we can survive without the use of an arm or a leg, while the blood flow is cut off, we can survive with an energetic tourniquet closing down our sexuality, emotions, or intuition.

After the wound is closed and the physical tourniquet is removed, the process of blood flowing back into the limb is intensely painful. If you've ever gotten cold enough that the circulation to your feet was reduced, then had your feet warm up quickly, you may also have some idea of how physically painful it is to have circulation returning.

Likewise, when we open up to wholeness, rather than agreeing to have parts of our being cut off and shut down, there can be pain when the life and energy begin to flow. Getting extra support in this process can be immensely helpful, even if it's just a friend who has the clarity to keep reminding you that the emotional rollercoaster is a healing process. Being alive includes pain. While we can learn to minimize suffering, the absence of any pain ever is a very bad sign.

I had an experience with a friend of a client who wanted very much to meet me. Since it seemed important to him, I told him about an event that I would be at and gave him the option of stopping by. From the moment he introduced himself, he had his hands all over me. It felt awful. I had all sorts of stories come up to disown my reaction. I told myself that since he was a friend of a client, to make myself look good as a professional, I needed to be gracious to him even though I was feeling "creeped out." I told myself that touching is within the standards of the metaphysical community and it would be rude to make a big deal. Of course, when I didn't ask him to stop, he touched me more and more.

Then I started with the indirect messages to try to get him to back off. I excused myself to the bathroom to get away, and when I came out he bought my book and asked me to sign it, leaning against me as I did and touching my hand while he gave me the pen. I grabbed my partner for a long kiss, using the non-verbal, "See, I'm taken," to no avail. Finally I left, feeling icky.

I was angry with him for not getting my subtle messages, and especially upset with myself for not telling him not to touch me. I simply couldn't think of a way that didn't sound mean and rude to say, "Please don't touch me." I brainstormed afterwards with some friends and came up with some things to say like, "Wow, your energy is really strong, it's a bit too intense for me when you touch me." So, I had a plan for what I would say, but I still felt awful.

I realized that by not enforcing that boundary, I had told my vulnerable sexual self that I couldn't be counted on to protect her. I valued looking good, being polite and not offending him above my own feelings. So, I sent him an email and told him, belatedly, how I felt about him touching me. The letter wasn't about making him bad, just about speaking my truth.

He never responded and that was fine with me. Writing it released the knot in my stomach, because it told my inner child that I would protect her. It also felt like a way that I had helped other women he might encounter. If he was coming from a place of integrity, he would take the information under advisement in dealing with women in the future. Most men I've spent time with would never want to make a woman sexually uncomfortable. Yet, it's too easy for a woman to do what I did and not speak up about what doesn't feel good. So, some men do things that don't feel good to women, simply because they never get honest feedback to tell them how it feels.

In either case, it was a great lesson for me. I walked away in integrity with my inner child, prepared to deal with the next person who crossed those lines. Oddly enough, once I come to that place, I often never need to put my plan into action. Somehow, I simply don't attract people who are trying to push the boundaries. Those who like to push boundaries generally have an amazingly well-honed, if unconscious, skill of knowing exactly where they can get away with pushing the limits and simply don't try to push the boundaries with people who give a clear, strong sense of self.

## Learning your own boundaries

During my kissing quest I sometimes let people kiss me and touch me even though I wasn't comfortable with them. My goal was to have other people initiate physical and mild sexual contact within this group of people I trusted. I set the guidelines of how they could touch, and in order to make it safe for everyone to approach me, I made a practice of greeting all kisses and cuddles in a positive fashion. It gave me the chance to feel pretty, admired, sought after.

But I wasn't sure how to say no to the members of the group who didn't feel good and safe to me, like one man who wanted his hands on my body while it felt like he disliked me personally. I was afraid of hurting his feelings and offending him, making him dislike me even more. I was concerned that if I became more selective, people would back away for fear of offending me.

I look back on this experience of making myself available to a touch that I didn't enjoy as something that was just where I was at the time. I made a choice to let someone touch me and kiss me a little to avoid hurt feelings, to avoid conflict, in an effort to manage people's perceptions of me. It was a discomfort, and one I decided I could live with then. This phase and experience was part of growing my discernment about sexual energy—this person's touch feels good, this person's doesn't.

I also know that this experience was part of what got me to the place of my stronger, more confident self today. We tend to see the failures, "Oh, I let him touch me and I didn't like it," instead of the successes. I was being present! I figured out in the moment that his touch didn't feel good. I didn't say anything at that moment, but afterwards I made plans to keep myself safe, whether it was going back and confronting the person about their behavior, asking other people to run interference, or just arranging to not be near someone who made me uncomfortable.

Today, I feel much greater ease saying no to someone. I was able to look a date in the eye over coffee and say, "Thanks so much for meeting me. While I think you're a great person, the sexual attraction just isn't there for me." I didn't like disappointing him, but it didn't ruin my day, either. Today, it feels more comfortable to say no and risk someone not liking me than endure a touch that doesn't feel good. In the healing steps I took to get to the place I am today I would let the safe but not so energetically enjoyable man kiss me because it felt safer and better to be touched than to have someone feel hurt or—horrors!—dislike me. This was a better step than avoiding all sexual contact as I'd done previously in order to feel safe. As I healed sexually, I was taking better care of myself, while also getting better and better at experiencing the pleasures of sex and intimacy.

## Chapter 7—Touch and Sex

One of the things I learned about myself as I explored my sexuality was how much I need and love to be touched. In fact, my need and desire to be touched, held, and caressed far exceeds my desire for sex. I love sex—the passion, the intensity, the pleasure. Other kinds of touch feed me in a deeper, subtler way, with sustained pleasure, intimacy, and enjoyment. Following the healing around my sexuality, sex and non-sexual touch can blend and flow together with greater ease, but when I was first learning about my sexuality it was complicated ground.

In certain cultures, people can be desperately hungry for touch. In my cultural upbringing, touch is usually reserved for romantic relationships, during sex, and between parents and young children. People are taught and learn cues about personal space from an early age. In the US, many people maintain very large bubbles of personal space, compared to other cultures. I remember my Spanish teacher telling the story of a man from the US visiting his uncle in Spain. His uncle kept coming into his personal bubble and the man kept backing up, until, in frustration, the uncle grabbed him and held him in place to talk to him.

If you have particularly touchy friends or come from a cultural background that embraces more physical contact, greeting and saying goodbye with a hug is pretty normal. But for many adults, being held and touched is something that is restricted to a sexual experience and/or a romantic relationship. I believe that many people meet their touch needs with sex. And, if you're healthy and there isn't a lot of trauma, this can be a perfectly good strategy.

## Learning how I wanted to be touched

I've had experiences with various men in which I stated a boundary about my sexual participation that they unfortunately ignored. (My boyfriend at sixteen was the worst offender. More on that below...) Once he had agreed to my terms, the man in question would proceed to touch me in pleasurable ways that did not include my breasts or genital area. It felt wonderful and I would relax into it, loving it, surrendering to it. Then the man would begin to push a boundary a little bit, brushing my breast or moving closer to the genital area. At that point I would freeze, beginning an inner dialogue of conflict with myself. If I told him "no," would he be unhappy with me? Would he stop the pleasurable touch? But now the touching didn't feel so good.

My boyfriend at sixteen added to my sexual trauma. Unless you explicitly agree to kink, anyone who yells at you in a nasty way during sexual activity, no matter how extensively and passionately he may apologize afterwards, is a dangerous choice for a lover, especially if it happens more than once. While we never had sex, we had enough sexual activity to allow me to explore many ways someone could pressure and manipulate me for sexual activity. My longing for touch and my fear of setting boundaries (because, yes, sometimes there was a negative reaction from him) were a big part of my allowing myself to be manipulated. The longing to be touched, to be special, to be loved, to have someone pay attention to me—along with the belief that I was somehow wrong for not wanting sex—were the elements that caused me to stay in that relationship for about six months, before deciding that being alone was better than that.

Setting boundaries in my teens and twenties were challenging for fear that the person would be upset or pull away. When I was in this relaxed, open-hearted place of having been touched, the fear of emotional withdrawal by the other person and my vulnerability were even greater. Furthermore, if I set a boundary, the touching might stop—and, remember, I desperately craved touch!

I would argue with myself, freezing and becoming hyper-vigilant at the same time, watching to see if the touch would escalate even further past the boundary that I had originally set. One the best gifts my first lover gave me was his incredible generosity with touch. He would hold me and stroke my skin for hours without ever having a goal of turning it sexual. It took me until I was nineteen to find him.

## The effects of molestation

Ongoing molestation often has the element of a child trading being touched in an awful way in order to get love and affection. I was lucky not to have that combination, but that type of energy played out when I began being sexual as a teenager and adult. Many of my clients who were molested explain that their abuser was also the only person showing love and affection to them as children. The lack of options and deep longing for love, combined with traumatic shame, may cause children to endure molestation. As adult survivors of childhood sexual trauma, we can find ourselves struggling to go through the motions or tolerating sex we really don't want in order to get the love, affection, attention, and touch that we crave.

I suspect that most of the readers of this book will be women, but for the men, a word on using non-sexual touch, such as massage and cuddling, as part of your seduction approach: It works. And there are many women who find a transition from that kind of touch to sex perfectly fine and enjoyable. After all, if your touch brings pleasure, the woman in your arms may want to experience a wider range of sensation. However, women who have unresolved sexual trauma can freeze in this situation. Make sure the woman actually says "yes" to sex, rather than just not saying "no." Otherwise she has the potential to leave the situation with bitter morning-after regrets and additional trauma. She may even consider it date rape.

## Enjoying non-sexual touch

During my kissing quest I naturally met a lot of new faces. I found a circle of people within the SCA who were available to hold me, cuddle me, and caress me to my heart's content with no sexual agenda. This is not to say that some of the people wouldn't be delighted to entertain me sexually; just that there is a world of difference between someone acting from that agenda versus someone who is able to enjoy the moment. One of the great gifts I now enjoy in my life is a whole circle of friends with whom I can exchange touching and cuddling without any thought of sex.

I tend to find goal-oriented sex rather dull. Some number of men (and women) are all about how efficiently the experience can be moved along to an orgasm for both parties. You miss so much amazing territory along the way. I enjoy men who have embraced the idea that sex doesn't automatically stop when the man has ejaculated. Unfortunately, few men espouse or even entertain this philosophy, and it is an idea that many never even heard suggested.

Likewise, goal-oriented touch just isn't my thing. I don't want someone to rub my shoulders or cuddle with me so that I'll relax, feel good with them, and decide to have sex. Today, I have more than a dozen people whom I trust completely never to push a cuddle session towards a sexual encounter. I can say to any of them, "I need to be held and touched" without raising a single eyebrow. In fact, we often end up in puppy piles with lots of people cuddling. I love it. I especially love being held in that way by men; it seems like there's an extra healing layer. Now, these gatherings often have a charge of sexual energy and that energy is simply allowed to be; it doesn't lead to sexual activities. My comfort level with sexual energy allows me to just relish that as part of the fabric of the event, without it leading to a sexual experience, just as my kissing seldom led to sex.

It took time to develop these relationships, and along the way, I found people in the same social group who just didn't get it on some level. I got good at being clear that not everyone had the same privileges of touch with me. When someone made the wrong assumptions and touched my body without invitation after seeing other people cuddle and hold me, I would just move away, let them know I wasn't comfortable, or find people I trusted to run some interference. Generally, the people I had those experiences with were people that many members of the group were finding problematic. It takes a unique group to understand touch for the sake of touch, rather than the sake of sex. And, when people reach that understanding, they often find how wonderful it is.

## Humans need touch—every day!

I forget sometimes how much I need touch, get busy with things, and find that no matter how much I am accomplishing, I feel unfulfilled. The best thing for filling up my loving cup, improving my mood, and feeling better is to make a date with someone to be held and cuddled. It may or may not include sex. The more tired I am, the more likely I am to just need to be caressed without sex. It's wonderful to have many options for this.

I invite you to consider what it would be like to actively cultivate non-sexual friendships that include a lot of touch. When you're starting out, agreeing not to have sex and holding to it can be very helpful. It helps if neither of you is distracted by the question of "Where is this going?" when touching and cuddling. You may find you have to wade through men who agree to touch without sex, then try to turn it sexual—get rid of those types immediately! You want to be able to relax and trust the people you're sharing this experience with. You can pick gay guys or other women (straight men are generally not up for cuddling other straight men).

If you're in a relationship with a partner who's not comfortable with you cuddling other people, talk about setting up some non-sexual touch and cuddle times. If your partner doesn't honor your boundary about it being non-sexual when that's clearly stated and reinforced, or if they get angry at the boundary, you may not be in the best or kindest relationship for yourself.

Sometimes having an additional distraction during this new way of closeness can be helpful. Watching a movie while cuddling can be a good combination. If non-sexual touch is something you haven't had a lot of, it can feel vulnerable and intimate and a bit uncomfortable at first, so watching a movie or blending it into something else can ease the intensity and make it more comfortable. During times when you're celibate, touch can be especially important. For example, I tend to spend some time not having sex after a major relationship ends, but being held and touched is very important to my healing process. For women who think they can't go without sex and want to, a lack of being touched enough may be part of this.

Cuddling and touching are nurturing and fulfilling for the inner child. Sex is not, so much, in my experience. So, if you're feeling vulnerable, needy, and craving love and affection, being touched and held is perfect. For me, having sex is not always something that is good or right for me if I'm feeling emotionally vulnerable. Sometimes it can be healing to open on that level to a partner when I'm feeling vulnerable in the relationship, but if I need nurturing, non-sexual touch is better. Today, sexual and non-sexual touch often flow together, weaving in and out when I'm with a lover. And there are still times when I ask friends who aren't lovers to hold me, and lovers just to cuddle without sex. For me to feel happy and balanced, more non-sexual touch is needed than sex itself.

## Chapter 8—Between Women

The heterosexual bias of my book became glaringly apparent to me the deeper I got into the writing of it. As a bisexual woman, I feel some measure of regret that this is so. The majority of my experience has been with men, and I can only write from my own experience, but I'd like to share a bit about my journey in regards to connecting with my sexual attraction to women.

My kissing quest afforded me my first kiss with a woman. It was an exciting experience to start with, as there was actually a line of people waiting to kiss me. This gorgeous, totally confident woman came up with a lovely man on a leash. First she had him kiss me, then asked if I'd like her to kiss me. She made it clear that I could accept or decline without any risk of giving offense.

When I accepted, I quickly realized that kissing a woman is different than kissing a man. Her lips were softer. She tuned in more completely and read my responses better——a phenomenon I noticed with the other women that followed. I also enjoyed the sexual charge surrounding kissing a woman for the bystanders. There's a focus and excitement of those watching that can flow into the experience. I know there are plenty of women who find this same voyeuristic energy annoying and invasive when they are sharing a mild sexual moment with their girlfriend, but for me, in this case, it was part of the richness of the energetic experience.

The woman in question wandered away with her decorative man in tow after a warm, lingering kiss, and I found myself wondering what it would have been like to spend more time with her.

Being the research-minded girl that I am, following that experience, I made a point of kissing women whenever the opportunity arose. I found that on average, women kiss better than men. Women seemed better able to meet me in the pure sensuality of the experience. Men who kissed me, no matter how clearly they understood that I would not share their beds, seemed distracted by that thought, nonetheless. Men often wanted more, while women seemed to simply enjoy the experience as complete in and of itself.

Eventually the universe provided me with the opportunity to have a few sexual experiences and relationships with women. I noted some of the thoughts and fears that came up. For one thing, being with a woman simply feels more vulnerable to me. I try longer and harder to make a woman emotionally happy and it feels more complicated. With men, much of the time just reflecting the fact that I adore them, delight in their company, and feel happy to be with them seems to ease male moodiness. A couple of my friends have shared the instant change in their husband's mood if they lift up their shirt or show off cleavage. That's not a trick that works with other women, in my experience.

## Hidden prejudice

One of the things I realized about myself which surprised me is my affinity for gender role dynamics. As an engineer and a feminist, I was surprised to note that one of my reservations about being with a woman related to the inability to play the "girl" card. I find it charming when a lover opens a door for me, lifts heavy things, or does something protective. It's a flavor I enjoy immensely when the man can play chivalry as a charming game, without entertaining any doubt about my competence as a human being. There are men who find running this kind of protective, gallant energy with a receptive woman delightful as well.

But just as that gendered yin and yang contrast has a sweetness to it, there are deep gifts derived from the experience of being with another woman. There can be a harmony and a deep intimacy; and it can be much easier to understand your partner. I adore men, but often I can't begin to understand their thought processes or predict their responses beyond a certain scope.

I tend to enjoy women more as people outside the realm of sexuality. I am more interested in their life experience, their stories, their aspirations, and their interpersonal process. Discovering the similarities and differences to me are fascinating. I'm interested in knowing, "How are you moving through this world in this female body?" So, blending that with a sexual passion can be breath-taking.

I recently ended up in bed with a woman who had been a friend for a couple of years. There had always been a sexual energy there, but I had not been prepared to initiate an actual sexual relationship. My fears came up. I feel like men are fairly simple to please in bed, but feared I would disappoint a woman. I valued the friendship and had the usual concern that perhaps adding in a sexual element would put that at risk. I felt more shy and nervous and vulnerable, as well as excited and aroused when I came to her bed for the first time. And yet, in terms of sheer, intense, physical and energetic pleasure, this lady consistently created an experience that was unsurpassed.

I'm still very much exploring this aspect of my sexuality. I feel more in control with men, more able to have things happen in bed on my terms. Yet, with sexuality, being completely in control and able to anticipate the outcome isn't always what leads to the most intensely pleasurable experiences of being able to just let go and enjoy. So, my understanding of what it means to be sexually attracted to women is still a part of myself that I am learning about and exploring.

## Healing the wounds between women

One of the pretty stories that I've heard told about the nature of women is the wonderful notion of their innate cooperation, mutual support, and love. It's a beautiful idea in theory, yet many women experience just the opposite. For many straight women, the most vulnerable experiences aren't with men, but with other women.

Pain and wounding can happen between girls in school, when a group of girls band together to tease or mock another girl. Women can engage in character assassinations and warfare in the work place. Granted, men and women clash at work, as do men with each other, but most of the stories I hear are of issues between women "telling" on each other and trying to make each other look bad or gossiping about each other. Working as an engineer and mostly with men, there just wasn't that much focus on the interpersonal aspects of who got on well with whom. The focus on the interpersonal can be a strength in the process of creating teams and consensus—or a liability for a woman spending a lot of energy engaged in a story of what others should or shouldn't do or how people perceive her.

I had a major challenge with a woman in my first job out of college. I was working as an engineer and she was working as a supervisor for the production line, so I technically outranked her. She was at least thirty years older than me and had worked with men in engineering her whole career, without a degree. At the time, I was terribly hurt by her efforts to control, dominate, and show me up. She came up with bizarre demands, like insisting that I use zip ties to put up work instructions rather than just clipping them up, even though they would be taken down half an hour later. It was the silliest thing, yet she put tremendous force of energy into making me do this and made it clear that she would fight me with everything she had to make sure I did what she stipulated as mandatory. I was deeply confused.

I finally realized that she had spent her whole life working to be respected and treated as an equal by men and to suddenly see me simply walking into a job where I had all of those things (and she didn't) was hard for her to witness. I hadn't paid the same dues she had in terms of sexism and, because I had a degree, I was in a higher paid and more prestigious position. I realized that if she controlled me and made me do what she said or got me in trouble with the management, she felt that somehow balanced the power for her. At the time, I was earnestly working very hard and trying to do my very best. Interoffice politics were something that I'd never experienced.

Now, many women who had paid similar dues of working to be recognized for their competence were excited and delighted to see me come into the work place with an engineering degree. In most of my professional career, I felt immensely supported by other women. But this experience demonstrated that not all women are naturally supportive of other women.

## Healing negative self-image

I notice that women do much more to sustain body hatred than men. Women hold their own internal harsh judgments of their bodies which, in turn, inevitably lead to harsh judgments of other women's bodies. While there are some men who are attracted to the "never too thin" standard, (and I wouldn't be all that sad if those men tumbled off a cliff one fine day), most of the obsession with size is by women. In fact, many men struggle to let a woman know they find her desirable, only to run into the impenetrable wall of her own negative self-perception.

While it is said that women compete, I find it's more about comparing. I always feel vulnerable when telling others of my foibles, failures, and struggles. I remember sharing an experience of a relationship in a women's studies class. It was a writing class and I included some of my journal entries about how stupid and wrong and bad and helpless I felt. It was the first time I'd opened that up to let other people see it. And I was shocked to have the other women in the group respond with love and joy and support and praise! Here I had spent years trying to show everyone how good and smart and able and strong I was to get them to love me, and they loved me more when I showed them my wounds.

In healing your relationship to yourself, in embracing your feminine self, and in being honored and supported in that, it's important to look at how you look at other women.

## Opening your heart

Toward the end of a six-month spiritual journey with a woman's group, we were talking about how we felt about women. During this journey, deep, profound bonds of love and trust had been developed. Nearly three years after the class ended, I still count those women as among my most precious friends. For me, the experience was about learning to really open my heart and experience intimacy with someone other than a lover. The comment was made and affirmed how some of the women in the group previously hadn't liked women, hadn't trusted them.

It turned out that another layer of that magical six-month journey was healing the ways that we each felt closed and suspicious of women. All the women in the class were beautiful, but several of them were blond-cheerleader-professional-model beautiful. These particular sisters activated deep healing for me, because they held up the mirror of my own insecurities about the pretty, popular girls and how they might judge me. If I wear Birkenstocks and they wear strappy, designer heels, will they think less of me? This was true only in my own mind, as it turned out.

Another of my sisters in the group has a lovely body that happens to be very much in alignment with our culture's view of the perfect shape and size. She shared with me how painful it was to be told in an angry way by another friend how she couldn't possibly understand what it was like to be overweight. That experience of activating and running into other women's jealousy, comparison, and insecurity was excruciating for her. In fact, for conventionally beautiful women, it can be hard for those around them to accept that they might have pain or problems.

Realizing the ways that your heart is closed or you feel insecure around other women is a quick way to point to areas that need more healing. Having connected with some conventionally beautiful women who are also wonderful, supportive, loving, admiring friends, I realized how much I missed out on by discriminating and telling unkind stories about women around whom I experienced my insecurities. They weren't judging me, I found; I was judging them first, sure that they would be judging me.

In my kissing quest, many women in monogamous relationships invited me to kiss their husbands. I got a free pass to cuddle, flirt, and play with men whose wives wouldn't have permitted this in general. I know that part of that came from the simple truth that I was more invested in how much fun the wife or girlfriend was having than in getting to play with her husband or boyfriend. Even if it was never stated, everything about how I played my game communicated to the women in question that I would not be careless of their feelings and needs. When in doubt, I always prefaced my kissing request with, "If it will not offend your wife or girlfriend…" I found an abundance of men to go around. I didn't need to compete for them.

Furthermore, as I got better at the kissing quest, I learned to share the energy and attention. If I had my arm around a girlfriend in a non-sexual way and was gathering sexual attention from men in the area, she could share in it. I got tremendous enjoyment from figuring out ways to get my female friends the male attention they were wanting.

The great thing is that as I heal my wounds about being around other women and become more open and less judgmental, I contribute energy to all women healing wounds that separate them from other women. Every time someone turns inside, finds compassion for herself and then for others, or creates enough safety to open her heart a little more, it contributes to universal healing.

# Chapter 9—Enjoying the Delightful Masculine

Part of my journey has involved falling in love with the Divine Masculine. It's sort of an odd thing to realize that for many years when I was making love to men, talking to men, and kissing men, I wasn't feeling a deep delight in the masculine. My assessment of whether I was safe with a given man often took precedence over enjoyment. I also felt a need to be loyal to a story that women were somehow better than men.

Oddly enough, being in a monogamous relationship with another woman for a year and a half deepened my appreciation for men. There were aspects that I loved about being with a woman; similarities of experience and deep connection, and I discovered that romantic relationships are complex regardless of gender. I was spending little time with men and most of my social time with women, which on one level was great since I adore women. Being romantically involved with a woman and surrounded primarily by women was a great opportunity to learn more about my longings for men. I found that I really missed the masculine!

During the demise of the relationship and in the time that followed, the experiences I'd had over the previous years began to come together in a new appreciation of men. I was on a new path of realizations. I attended a workshop called "Making Sense of Men" (see the Classes and Workshops section at the end of the book for information about this free seminar). What I had observed anecdotally was presented in a lively, well-researched seminar that allowed me to see and name the patterns that I had found and heard expressed by the men who have touched my life.

## Misleading stereotypes

You may recognize that our society tells stories about how men are stupid, just out for sex, shallow. These stories are so pervasive that I simply assumed that all the men I was meeting—in my engineering job, in my dating life, and in my social groups of friends—were just exceptionally superior to the hypothetical "average" man. From what was stated in the seminar, and after talking to many, many men, I now understand that I was meeting the "average" man. In fact, the men I met often prefaced answers to my questions by stating that they didn't think they were typical, then proceeded to give the same answer I'd heard from most of other men I'd asked. Even men have been brainwashed about other men!

I had already had occasion to question certain beliefs. For example, when I started dating, I thought men would jump at the chance to have a casual sexual relationship. I was shocked when I got turned down for sex without commitment. I had a number of men state that they would love to see where things went, spend time with me, and explore a relationship, but they weren't interested in just playing. They asked me to please call them if and when I wanted to be more than just casual lovers. Others agreed to the casual relationship but made it clear that they really wanted more. This difference of desire was ultimately a source of tension that ended some nice connections.

## How men connect

When men are emotionally engaged with women, they tend to do things instead of saying things. Men strive to take action to make the women they care about happy. Men express their feelings by attempting to contribute to and improve the life of the woman they love. They make time to spend with her and want to protect her. In fact, these are behaviors that last as long as a man is emotionally engaged with a woman, not just through the courtship phase. These are behaviors that men exhibit towards women they are responding positively to in any aspect of their lives, not just their romantic partners. This is how men really want to treat women!

So why don't we experience what they are trying to give to us? I realized that I, like so many women, was missing signs and indicators of ways that men in my life were emotionally engaging and attempting to contribute to my life and make me happy. I didn't recognize these efforts because they just didn't look like a woman's contribution of emotional support, kind words, compliments or active listening. With men, a contribution can take the form of advice, performing physical labors, or problem solving. In fact, as I applied this new lens, I could see ways that many men I had encountered (aside from those who were deeply wounded and those who were deeply angry with women) exhibited this kind of behavior towards all women.

Men who had happy mothers or experiences of feeling successful with women in romantic relationships are more adaptable across the gender gap. They are better able to read between the lines and not take women's emotional cycles personally. However, when men have been deeply wounded, feeling like they always fail with women, they will often withdraw at the first sign of unhappiness in their partner. For me and most of the women I know, feeling one's partner pull back and withdraw stirs up all manner of abandonment and "he doesn't love me" feelings. Hence, both people suffer, get confused and misinterpret the other person's wounds as a lack of love.

## The wounded and/or unavailable man
A man who has a low opinion of women, who finds them selfish, manipulative, and stupid, etc., likely has deep wounds related to women. You may find yourself in the dubious position of being "special;" not like those other bitches or whores. It can feel like being honored. However, since you are the nearest woman, you are likely to end up the target of whatever anger that man has towards women. Someone who doesn't like women has likely been wounded by them, and in an intimate relationship the partner is the person with whom that wounding will be brought up for healing. Not that I haven't been

the moth to the particular flame of the wounded man with the lovely light and good heart. I'm just noting that my wings got singed there.

Likewise, there are men who are simply walking a path in the world that is solitary in nature. They are expressing the energy of the monk, the hermit, the priest. It is a good and valid path, but in today's society there isn't a clear way to walk that path, and these men often seek relationship. They simply don't have the energetic wiring that causes them to respond in the usual way of having a deep desire to please women and make them happy. They are not compelled by their deepest nature to give, because their energy is directed into the solitary life, even when they marry. This man can be enticing, with a solidness and a spiritual nature. However, if a woman needs affection, attention, sex, and companionship to a significant degree, these men can feel painfully distant. Then again, for a woman expressing a similarly internal journey, such a man can be the perfect mate.

Another variation on the wounded man is the one who appears to hold women as incompetent, weak, and in need of male protection. Opening doors, lifting boxes, and other efforts to take care of women quickly change from charming to condescending when this attitude is present. The men who deny the strength, power, and capability of women are engaged in making women small so they can feel big. This may come from insecurity and a sense of being unlovable at the core; a deep feeling that a woman would never want him unless she needed him, so the wounded man paints women as needy and incompetent. Or, perhaps it is a symptom of an overall bully mentality. Either way, I've never found it an attractive characteristic and it's one that may compel a woman to close herself to support from all men.

## Signs of pleasure
Let's return to the middle of the spectrum. When an average guy is emotionally drawn to a woman, he feels compelled to exert himself to please and assist her. When a man opens a door for a woman or tries to help in some way (even if that way isn't needed or appropriate to the situation) it can be viewed as reflecting a belief that women are less able. But, to me it feels truer and more peaceful to see that many men

are simply delighted and emotionally compelled by women in general. There are many men who go out of their way to help women, to try to make them happy, to please them, to contribute, to protect them, not because they have a goal, but because it is their natural response. For some men it is specific to certain women, for others more general.

It was interesting to note how often men will take action to please me. One could argue that there's a deep agenda in every action to see if they can get me into bed (and I'm sure that's the motivation for some). I've also seen men deeply satisfied with simply having my attention, getting my smile, by my acknowledging and valuing their contribution. The more I work shamanically, the more clearly I see that there's a part of men that just seeks the approval, happiness, and pleasure of women, and to be acknowledged as contributing to that pleasure. It's not that men don't also love sex and dinner and other things from women; but you might be amazed at how often men say and mean, "Whatever makes her happy is fine with me."

My stories and fears of men got in the way of seeing this truth about how many men simply wanted to contribute to my happiness. I attributed hidden agendas and was reluctant to take energy offered to me. I get uncomfortable when men (well, people really, but let's focus on men for the moment) give to me. I feel like I owe it to them to like them or give them sex, so mostly I don't let them give. I feel guilty if they spend money on me or give more energy and attention than I'm offering. I feel this uncomfortable and miserable sense of owing them. It makes me reluctant to ask for what I want, both because of a fear of hearing "no," and a fear of what I will owe them. At the same time, I have a deep and tremendous longing to receive. I love to be touched, held, paid attention to, fussed over. If I can relax into it and trust the man, it feels wonderful when he picks up the check, pays attention to my physical comfort or drives me somewhere.

I realized how I trip myself up. I long to receive and yet, when a man tries to give to me, I often tell him "no." I let him know that I don't need whatever he's offering. I have this belief that if a man gives to me, he will find me too much trouble and so he'll like me better if I don't let him spend money or give me a foot rub. Yet, the opposite is truer, as most men feel best when their gifts are received and valued.

## What a man wants

In the "Making Sense of Men" seminar I attended, we learned about the feminine qualities that men are attracted to emotionally (as opposed to sexually). These include things like self-confidence, authenticity (i.e. the woman really means what she says and says what's on her mind), and passion for something in life. The last quality discussed in the seminar was receptivity. I realized that while I (mostly) have great self-confidence, passion, and authenticity, my receptivity is very limited. When men are met with a lack of receptivity to what they try to give, they tend to withdraw emotionally. Here I was trying to be low maintenance and undemanding by saying, "no, that's okay, I don't need that" in the hopes of being more loved, and it was instead pushing the man away.

When a man meets a woman he's drawn to emotionally, he is likely to try to contribute, protect, and make her happy. If these efforts are met with delight and receptivity, he continues to engage and often keeps making moves to deepen the relationship. Men tend to withdraw when their efforts at making a woman happy begin to fail. When she is unhappy and asking him for things he doesn't understand or know how to do, he begins to pull away and focus on not being in trouble rather than making her happy.

Have you ever wondered why nice men are drawn to women who are falling apart and needing help? Consider that it has a lot to do with the man's contributions being acknowledged and valued. This need to be needed, to contribute, to make a woman's life better, runs deep in many men. One of my long-time friends is simply delightful to be around because he is happiest and most deeply fulfilled when he is enhancing the life of a woman in some way. It's a deep and fundamental part of who he is, whether that woman is his lover or not.

This doesn't mean that as a woman it is wise, appropriate, or necessary to accept the gifts of time, energy, or advice that the men we meet in all aspects of our lives are eager to offer. Some of them come with strings, and some of them are from men we don't want to engage with even for a moment. Sometimes it would be taking advantage of someone's feelings to accept a gift.

I remember being taught as a child to say "Thank you" for a gift that was disappointing and uninteresting to me, as well as for those I liked. It was good manners to acknowledge that another person had gone to some effort to please me. I wasn't required to ultimately keep the gift or play with it, but I was expected to acknowledge the gift.

Even when the attempt to please is wildly off base, there is a healing that takes place between men and women every time a woman can say "Thank you" for an effort to contribute or please. This could be a piece of unsolicited advice, a suggestion for a solution to a problem, an offer to buy dinner or an effort to spend an afternoon. Even if it is, "Thank you so much, I'm not available to accept that," there's still a healing between the genders in the acknowledgement.

## Enjoy receiving from the masculine

For the woman, the healing is about taking a moment to see that a man is responding to her in a positive way, demonstrating his desire to please. It can make her feel special, important, seen, and valued. To have another person pay us the compliment of going out of his way to try to make our lives better and to connect with us can feed the parts of our egos that long for approval and acknowledgement. When a woman feels unattractive, she often fails to see the gifts she is being offered. The apparent rejection of the masculine generosity deepens the gulf between the sexes, while perpetuating her misconception that she is unattractive.

For men, the healing happens from being acknowledged by the feminine. Too many men are wounded as children when they express their nature by trying to make their mother happy and contribute to her. If Mom is distracted or unhappy or missing these efforts, a deep sense of failure in regards to women can be created. If a woman can see, value and acknowledge a man's efforts to give, even without accepting the gift, she offers him a chance to heal, and he is more likely to be open to giving to the next woman.

I believe this is the explanation for why three of my lovers who expressed a deep longing for primary partners went on to connect with the women they subsequently married, within six months of spending time with me. In each case, they were experiencing a "dry spell" of not having a woman in their lives for years before we connected. I just enjoyed them and valued them and I believe that experience of success was part of what made them open enough to connect with their life partners.

## Feeling attractive and safe

The journey to where I am now has a lot to do with feeling safe enough that I'm not so shy or caught up in my fears, allowing me to see when someone reaches out and to respond accordingly. I'm no longer so much in my own story of how I'm not attractive or men aren't safe, that I overlook when a man goes out of his way for me, like the guy at the juice counter giving me twice as much wheat grass juice as I ordered. I love being adored, so it makes my life happier when I see how men are admiring me and going out of their way to catch my eye, contribute to my day, or to please me. The kissing quest was a great place to see how much men enjoy a woman's sexual attention and energy, even knowing that they are unlikely ever to have sex with her.

To my great surprise, I found my personal myth about men didn't agree with reality when it came to what men find sexually attractive. It is funny to recall and interpret past events from my present understanding. I had experiences of men trying to catch my eye and doing just about everything except skywriting to indicate that they were attracted to me. Those efforts often failed utterly against my complete conviction in my own lack of attractiveness and ignorance of how a man behaves when he is interested.

My experience is that far more men are attracted to all different sizes than people realize. Men with old souls especially tend to find women with more curves more desirable. Over and over again, I see that it is not that men aren't attracted to women of size; rather, many curvier women are so sure they're not attractive that no amount of attention will dislodge that belief.

This was an area where having good friends really helped. I had people point out to me when men were drawn to me and compelled by me and striving to get my attention. I was out one evening with my lovely younger sister, and at the end of the evening she pointed out that many guys had tried to talk to me; I was just too shy to talk back, so they gave up. Being sexy and getting men to notice me and want my attention wasn't the problem; my failure to notice their efforts and talk to them was the problem.

## You are attractive—believe it!

It causes the men who love us great pain when we, the women they love and find wonderful, desirable, and sexy, beat up on ourselves. They know we're attractive, they desire us, and it's very painful to watch us tie ourselves in knots over not being thin enough or whatever petty perceived flaw we agonize over. The men who love us want us to be happy; more than that, they want to make us happy, so it's doubly painful when we hurt ourselves with self-criticism about our lovely, feminine bodies.

Of course, there are men who are only attracted to a very particular physical type. There are even men who will try to force their partners into that type. While I can theoretically recognize that this comes from wounds, I feel not at all compelled to spend time helping those disagreeable men with the aforementioned wounds. There is, in these men, a failure to honor the feminine divine embodied in women, and I experience outrage to witness them dishonor that which I know to be sacred.

I have the best experiences of being with men who fundamentally adore women. They think women are lovely and soft and pretty. I feel most relaxed and confident with a man who I know likes women of all shapes and sizes. If a man comments about fat women being unattractive, no matter how much evidence of his intense devotion and attraction to me, I will never feel as confident and pretty around him.

I find that many, many more men find women beautiful, desirable, and wonderful, regardless of shape and size. They get blocked and tripped-up and dismissed by our own failure to recognize how sexy and desirable we really are. With a few unworthy exceptions, more often it is women, not men, who condemn women's bodies for not meeting some impossible standard.

Through the kissing quest, it was empowering to realize how desirable I really am. By kissing anyone who made himself available, rather than deciding who was desirable and who wasn't, I had a chance to really see what a high percentage of men responded to me sexually. We often focus on one man and when he doesn't see us, we ignore the twenty who did.

In determining whether we are attractive to the opposite sex, we need to take in all the data. As an engineer, I think of it as setting up an experiment about whether plants grow under certain conditions, then ignoring and denying all the growth unless it was a leaf on the left side of the plant, three-quarters of the way up the stalk. The plant could have tripled in size, but I've decided not to see that as growth unless it's that one leaf where I happen to be looking at the time.

Feeling like one is truly attractive is something that may take time to nurture. I still have days when I freeze in a social setting because I've tripped over feeling too fat, too tall, and/or tongue-tied. But it happens less and less. And when I'm feeling sexy, confident, and desirable, men respond to me as sexy, confident, and desirable. When I'm feeling not so sexy, confident, and desirable, men still respond to me, but when they smile at me, or say hello, or try to start a conversation and I don't respond, they note that I'm attractive but not receptive and move on.

It's kinder to oneself, and to the men of the world, not to assume that they are judging us. Men find us desirable because we're women. It's not true for all men, but in my experience it's true for most men.

Try walking in the world with this understanding that men will be drawn to you simply because you're a woman and take their admiration as a gift. It isn't a gift that means you owe anyone or must spend time or energy; just a gift of a compliment when someone pays extra attention to serving you in a restaurant or smiles or says hello. This attitude will attract more men to admire and appreciate the way you decorate the world with your light and form.

If our expectation is that we will be met with approval, it's easier to relax, value ourselves, trust that we are desirable, and receive from the men we choose to invite into our lives. Just because someone admires you doesn't mean you need to take him home, but there is a gift that is held by the men who casually brush our lives.

Given how intensely, passionately, and single-mindedly most men are attracted to women—especially any woman who is interested in them—it seems a terrible waste that a woman would feel unattractive. Admitting and cultivating that sense of our own beauty also makes it less of an uphill battle for the men in our lives. We can take the gift of their admiration, trust in it, and receive the energy that they want to give us.

# Chapter 10—Dealing With Uncomfortable Feelings About Men

An experience of abuse or trauma can create a sense of fear around men. As an energetically sensitive, large-breasted teenager, I received a substantial amount of sexually-charged attention, ranging from surreptitious glances, to hooting calls and stares, to attempts at inappropriate touch by men of all ages. Every time I felt noticed in this way, my personal alarm bells went off even if nothing was actually done or said. I thought it was because I was shy that I got so panicky when I was alone with an older man. Such experiences were so overwhelming that I learned to block out any awareness of men finding me sexually attractive, which eventually evolved into my assumption that men in general weren't attracted to me.

During the kissing quest, I had the opportunity to invite sexual energy back into my personal arena on very specific terms. It was scary and exciting and highly charged. Sometimes I had more fun recounting my experiences to my friends than actually kissing men. It allowed me to explore each experience and receive praise and encouragement from someone who was willing to tell me over and over and over, "See, this is evidence of what I've been telling you all along: men find you pretty and sexy, but you just don't always notice."

Today I no longer go into a panic when a man looks at me. On a walk at a nearby lake, I saw a highly decorative man biking in the other direction, and without a thought I looked at him and smiled. He turned his head and said, "Hi, there" in an admiring voice. I walked on, warm and flattered at this moment of being admired. A few years ago, I would have been uncomfortable walking in public, careful to avoid eye contact, and I would have felt fear as well as excitement about a man looking at me. It was a wonderful moment to notice that my new instinctive response was openness rather than alarm.

## Recognizing old patterns

While the kissing quest allowed me not to feel threatened by strange men or sexual energy in and of itself, there are still men who trigger that old fear and panic. For example, I remember being at a metaphysical retreat with one such man. He had always treated me with the utmost courtesy, and I could clearly see his loving heart and deep desire to be loved. It seemed that with all the open-hearted, loving work the group was doing at the seminar, he still felt like the child out in the snow, looking in through the window, rather than someone receiving the same gifts of warmth and community as the rest of us. My goal was to hold compassion for him, yet I found myself experiencing an intense, at times overwhelming, desire to avoid him. I realized I was being triggered, so I took a deeper look at the situation.

The ironic thing was that at the time, I longed to be seen as beautiful, sexy and desirable in my curvy, ample body, and of all the men there, this man was the one who saw me most clearly as divinely beautiful. In talking circle and at the meals, he shared some of his past. He spoke of his mother with anger and bitterness, and it became clear that his relationships with women had brought him great pain that he hadn't resolved. I came to realize that the man in question held a deep anger at the Divine Feminine. On the one hand, he revered and honored the goddess, while on the other hand, he felt rejected by her and was angry and hurt. Once I put my finger on it, I was able to relax in his presence. That kind of anger is hard to deal with in anyone, but once I understood it, I could also know that I wasn't in "danger" and could relax my protective shields and be more compassionately present with him. Softening toward him allowed my heart to open, bringing a healing for both of us in which I could receive his awe of my beauty and he could feel honored by a woman he admired.

## Recognizing others' pain

When a man holds deep anger at women and/or unbalanced sexuality, women who are in tune with their deeper instincts experience this as a threat and a danger. This sense was profoundly amplified by being a victim as a child, but I also believe it is a deep survival instinct that all women have. Unfortunately, what I've seen of those who grow up being victimized repeatedly within the family of origin, is that this instinct gets shut down as unhelpful white noise. It then follows that we are attracted to those with similar imbalances in an unconscious effort to repair the pain from growing up. So for some women with extensive sexual trauma, healing is needed for them to learn to listen to those natural instincts.

I had a strong reaction when a particular new client called me. From the moment I spoke with him on the phone, I was having thoughts about whether it was safe to meet him, although we had a perfectly normal, very brief conversation, with nothing that indicated a problem. When the man arrived for his session, I was uncomfortable from the moment he walked in the door. Instead of the strong, clear voice I generally use, my voice came out sounding young and unsure. I'd been doing inner child work that day and I was very aware of how frightened that part of me was at that moment.

As we spoke, he explained his history of having been molested by a female relative and how his father and brother had molested other children. This was a devastating history, and once I entered shamanic reality, I could see that while this man wasn't a child molester or sexual predator, his sexuality was distorted by being victimized and by having his male role models display unhealthy sexual manipulation and aggression. The guides brought in the demi-god Pan to work with him on the pure, healthy expression of male sexuality, while I worked to bring back his soul parts and repair the extensive damage.

As soon as I understood that the feelings I had were a valid response to his energy, but didn't reflect an actual danger of abuse to me or others, I could relax. Instead of telling the part of myself that was trying to warn me of danger that it was wrong, I could say, "Yes, you are right, I know, and he's not a threat."

Too often as women we struggle to suppress an inconvenient feeling, thus disconnecting from our truth. This means that the feelings get stronger and more intense, because we're not listening, so we struggle harder not to feel them. This process makes it hard to make empowered choices about how we interact with the people around us. If we allow the feelings, even if we don't understand them, instead of struggling to get rid of them, we have more attention to deal with whatever the situation is more clearly and efficiently.

In the case of this client, my intuition about the sexual imbalance was dead on, but my feelings and intuition could only report that this might be dangerous. I needed my mind to sort through my experience of his normal behavior, my intuition, and his story. As healing occurs, it becomes easy to balance intuition with the rational process and set them to working together, rather than arguing with each other.

## Going into your fears

As I began releasing my attachment to stories about men being bad, selfish, not evolved, childish, or stupid, the next layer of my personal work arose: my fear of men came up. As I began taking a deeper look at the men in my life and asking the classic Byron Katie question, "Is this true?" I saw that the men I deal with are not cruel, thoughtless, unkind, or any of those persistent stereotypes. I noted the men in my life who are kind and generous, protective and loving, and suddenly I was feeling terribly afraid of faceless, dangerous men.

For example, I was getting ready for bed one evening and heard someone in the house next door screaming verbal abuse, "You fucking whore, I'm sick of you…" There were noises that could have been someone being hit. So, I called 911 to report it. I was then overwhelmed with my fear. What if the man guesses it was me who called the police? What if he threatens me? What if he attacks me? All my fear of the unbalanced, dangerous men came rushing to the surface. I made plans for denying it if anyone asked about who called the police. I read in my bedroom with a flashlight because I was too wound up to sleep and afraid that if he saw the light on next door, he'd put two and two together. I ran down the list of the many men in my life whom I could rely on to protect me and warn him off if he threatened me.

Something shifted in my sleep and by the time I woke up in the morning, I was back to my usual sense of feeling safe in the world. What occurred the night before had been a huge departure from my usual behavior and thought patterns. I felt what it is like to dwell in the fear of a violent man, one who doesn't care about the consequences, who could hurt me. This experience came up as part of what my guides called my fear detoxification as I released my stories about men as stupid, bad, and childish.

I talked to my guides about this seemingly illogical juxtaposition. Here I was feeling more loving and honoring towards the masculine, valuing it more, not telling myself the old "Men are bad or stupid" stories, and I was also feeling more vulnerable and afraid of male anger in my dreams and wandering thoughts. For the first time in my life, I was feeling safe to make eye contact with men and smile instead of looking away and avoiding, and that was feeling good. But where were these three a.m. fears coming from?

My guides said that being present with the feelings of fear and victimization was a critical part of releasing all the dark thoughts that I had bottled up about men. Avoiding that fear and ignoring it had accumulated a toxic build up. Now that I was addressing my feelings about the masculine, all my feelings were in play.

## Why we believe these stories

Through this process, I realized that part of the reason we tell our stories about men being bad is to avoid vulnerability. In terms of emotional vulnerability, both men and women often seek to protect themselves by running down the opposite sex with "women are crazy" and "men are pigs". We make perceived rejections and failed relationships feel less personal this way. If there's something fundamentally wrong with men/women, then there's not something fundamentally wrong with me that I keep failing to get what I want in relationships. It's a classic human defense that we apply in many areas of our lives.

But for women, this need to tell stories of men as bad, silly, childish, or stupid, this need to make fun of men, is also a way of mitigating our fear of the unbalanced, dangerous men we know to be out there. I don't believe there are many women who haven't either themselves been the victim of some male violence or known someone who has. Plus, movies and the nightly news underscore how dangerous men can be and how vulnerable women are. Laughing at what you're afraid of, making it silly, stupid, or contemptible in some way takes its power away. Just as common wisdom tells people afraid of speaking in public to picture the audience in their underwear, women have learned that mocking men is a way to feel less vulnerable.

Like so many defensive strategies, this one works after a fashion in allowing women to reduce fear of men in their daily lives. The downside is that we cut ourselves off from all the valuable things men offer—we can't regard them as overgrown children and simultaneously create relationships where we can lean on them for support, good advice, or loving attention. This disempowering worldview of men precludes being able to see the strength, power, and wisdom of our men.

## Making a change
My guides talked to me about not taking my fear so seriously, about making friends with it, allowing it to be, without judgment, and learning to breathe through it. They said that so much of the self-sabotaging behavior that human beings engage in is about avoiding the fear of the experience of being human. It is vulnerable to be in a human body; we are subjected to disease, illness, loss of loved ones, emotional rejection, and physical violence. We know that we can't control the world and sooner or later we will die, so we spend huge amounts of our energy creating our illusions of safety; engaging in a range of addictive behaviors, drama, and time-filling pursuits to avoid the fear that comes from the vulnerability of being human.

For example, one of the reasons that self-criticism is so addictive is that it is an attempt to control the self, thereby creating a distraction from how uncontrollable the larger world is. Condemning ourselves because we've said unkind things about ourselves also distracts from the fear of the vulnerability of being human.

So, my guides said that as this fear of violent, dangerous men arises, just be with it. I find I have to work to stay present with my fear, as with any shadow emotion. First of all, I have many defenses in place to distract myself from even noticing consciously that there's an uncomfortable emotion. I find that I'm just grabbing something sweet, or jumping online to see what fun emails I might have. Once I figure out that I'm masking an emotion and decide to stay with it instead of avoiding, then the real work begins.

I sit with the emotion, putting my attention lightly on it, and allow it to be. Then my awareness skitters off to something else—fantasy land, what I should be doing around the house, anything else that could distract me now. Then I come back, breathe deeply, and sit with the emotion some more. Perhaps new emotions arise, such as sadness and anger. Eventually, even if there are tears and some very uncomfortable moments, I'm left shaking my head. I fought *that* so hard? Sure it wasn't my favorite experience, but I feel so great afterwards and the suffering of feeling my feelings just isn't enough to justify the avoidance I put into it. It is in no way unusual for an emotionally miserable evening that I work through to be followed by an absolutely wonderful day the next day.

As we detox layer after layer of the fear and pain we have suppressed and avoided, it leaves our bodies and our energy fields. Without a reservoir of terror and pain, our intuition of what is a dangerous situation becomes more accurate and focused. We aren't using vast amounts of our energy to suppress the feeling. In addition to all the other benefits, this new space, lightness, and relaxation we exude as we learn to process our fear instead of fighting it is profoundly attractive to men. When women simply meet men as human beings, rather than seeing them all as potential predators, men can feel safe to offer the gifts of time, attention, and energy toward pleasing us.

# Chapter 11—Navigating Connections With Men

While most sexual predators are men, most men are not sexual predators. Figuring out how to navigate this truth can be a bit of work for women, especially those who have experienced some kind of sexual trauma.

Most of the men I know have good, generous hearts. They go out of their way to serve their community, to help and protect other people. These men have earnest good intentions where women are concerned, and would never put their sexual desires ahead of a woman's feelings and well-being.

In fact, nearly all the men I know will gleefully pontificate on their recommended approach to castrating and killing anyone who assaults a woman. Men feel a deep horror at sexual violence and anger at their powerlessness to stop it. It is painful for them, knowing that their mothers, sisters, daughters, wives, and lovers are at risk.

If you ask a group of men and women to remember the last time they felt their physical safety threatened, men might have to go back years to come up with an experience. For a number of women, the last time was in the past twenty-four hours. It can be hard for men to relate to women's fears. They say men's worst fear when it comes to women is that women will laugh at them. Women's worst fear when it comes to men is that men will kill them.

## Finding intelligent compassion

So, for the average man, who, like most, would never harm or attack a woman and who doesn't deal with fear for his own safety on a regular basis, it can be hard for his frame of reference to include what women experience. In fact, he may find it insulting and wounding when a woman has her fear of the violent masculine stirred up in his presence. While I'm particularly sensitive to the pain that women experience, I am also aware that there is no "good" experience for anyone in regards to sexual violence; everyone gets the short end of the stick. Somehow men deal with having the projection of predator or potential predator placed on them, although I imagine it takes a toll. It is painful for any human being to have their good, honorable intentions viewed with suspicion and misinterpreted.

My path has been about learning to take care of my own feelings and need for safety first. As I get better at that and have energy and attention left over, it leaves me free to hold compassion for the point of view of the men who are paying a terrible price for the violence against women.

I particularly appreciate when a man demonstrates an understanding of the vulnerability that women often experience in regards to men. I appreciate when a man offers his number instead of asking for mine, makes a point of walking me to my car, and expects I will need to get to know him before getting into a car with him or inviting him to my home. That kind of sensitivity is a great way to make a good impression on a first date. On the other hand, if a man gets his feelings hurt because my rule is to get to know him before telling him where I live, I take that as a huge, flashing warning sign. It doesn't necessarily indicate that he is a potential stalker, but it does show a lack of empathy, awareness, and emotional maturity.

## Trust your intuition

So as women, how do we navigate these waters? At some point most women cross paths with predators, either directly or through violence against a close friend or family member. Unfortunately, our society doesn't teach women good ways to spot predators. In some ways, our culture teaches women to be safe through confinement. We are told to stay indoors, always have someone with us when walking at night, and not open the door to strangers. We learn that in public space, especially if alone, we are vulnerable and should be vigilant.

Despite the fact that most rapes are by someone the woman knows, we learn more about protecting ourselves from strangers than about reading the signs of the predator or abuser among the people we know. Women, socially conditioned to please, are taught from a young age to "be nice" and put their feelings aside. So, when we feel uncomfortable and our intuition starts screaming, "Danger! Danger!" we often suppress it.

Developing a feeling of being safe with and around men is something that may happen slowly and takes time. Again and again, I see that the more I honor, enjoy, and appreciate the men in my life, the more generously and openly they give to me. I am also fully aware that my caution in deciding whether I'm safe with a given man is valid and good. My being healed and open to the masculine doesn't mean that all men are safe.

My healing has allowed my intuition to become more focused. Instead of reacting with fear to being alone with any man (as I did as a child and teenager), only some men set off alarm bells. I know that only a small percentage of the men I react to with alarm are truly dangerous and, at the same time, I'm not interested in getting close enough to discover whether this one is truly dangerous or just wounded in regard to women.

The kissing quest was powerful for me in transmuting my fears related to men, especially sexually aroused men. I played this game in the company of friends, knowing that if anyone ever tried to push my limits, held onto me when I didn't want to be held or was even rude, my friends would promptly intervene. So, I had this beautiful, special space to be sexual, to connect with men and know that I was going to be completely physically safe at all times. And somewhere in the laughter, flirtation, flattery, and kisses, much of my fear of men blew away like smoke.

## Develop a personal scale

For women, the balance is not simply to go into the world putting aside all their fear about men. Rather, we learn to apply the right amount of concern to the perceived level of danger. It is best if we don't step into the elevator (i.e., an enclosed, largely sound proof box) with the man who gives us the creeps, just so we don't hurt his feelings. Odds are we'd step out of the elevator okay, but it is not wise to take the risk.

During a trip to Hawaii where I was leading a retreat, I had the most amazing day. I felt clear and good in my role as facilitator, in complete harmony with the land and blissful in the energy. And, while we danced on the side of the volcano and connected to spirit, someone broke into the car and stole our laptops and a purse. There were many lessons and gifts, but one of them was a reminder that no matter how spiritual and connected I am, no matter how high and clear my vibration, I'm still living in the physical world with people who are not safe to me or my possessions. I still need to be mindful of the physical world.

Healing yourself doesn't get rid of your fear of violent men; what it does give you is the correct and proportionally balanced fear that accurately reflects the danger. It causes you to deal with the physical world as needed—whether it is taking a self-defense class, getting an escort to walk you to your car, or just being more alert to the world around you, so that you don't have to be afraid all the time and can go on about your life. It causes you to value your own feelings of danger above the potential pain to the ego of a man with whom you are faced.

## Opening to men

When women feel safe, we can open our energy and light and let it shine. This allows men to approach us, admire us, seek to please us, and make us happy. It is not merely the men we attract as lovers, but the men from all areas of our lives. We have the chance to enjoy and savor the fact that men are powerfully attracted, charmed, and compelled by us.

In dealing with men, of whom some very small percentage are abusers, sexual predators, and stalkers, it is important to recognize that most men are none of those things, not even a little bit. I've experienced too many conversations wherein a normal man is blamed for the violence that women experience. Despite knowing that the man in question would never cross those lines, I've heard him blamed for being male, for wanting to have sex with women, or for not having a deep enough empathy for what it is like to be at risk for that kind of violence.

It is easy for the deep anger and pain to get misdirected. It is important to realize that we can't take an average and blame every man we meet for being some percentage abuser. In the interest of safety, it is sometimes necessary to treat all men with caution. But treating all men with anger and blame is unjust. While I am inclined to hold men accountable when they show a significant lack of empathy for what it is to be a woman who is vulnerable to violence, from a place of integrity I must also consider what it is like for a man to be tarred with the "predator" brush despite his innocence.

# Chapter 12—The Ouchy Stuff

There is a great scene in the movie, "Something's Got to Give," in which the main character, having had her heart badly broken, is alternately typing furiously with a delighted look on her face because her writing is inspired and bawling her eyes out because it hurt, it hurt, it hurt. That was my experience with one of my break ups.

For me, the significant silver lining was the inspiration to write about the experience because looking at how much it hurts when a relationship ends is not something I care to think about on an average, pleasant day. Yet, the times when I really hurt are some of the most authentic and transformative. I meet myself in new and deeper ways. I connect to my strength, power, and courage. I can let go of not-so-helpful patterns that I had for avoiding pain, because I'm already in pain.

One of the moments when things really clicked for me was listening to a Zen practitioner describe what she called the primal wound of being human. Being in physical form, constrained by the boundaries and sense of self as individual, can result in a wound that comes from the illusion of separation.

## Veils of separation

The human experience offers many wonderful opportunities such as the chance to experience emotion and for creation to see itself. In order to do that, we incarnate with these veils of separation, allowing us to believe and experience ourselves as fundamentally different from the person next door or someone on the other side of the world. In spirit form, we know we are all connected; the illusion of separateness doesn't exist. While this is simply part of what is needed to have the physical experience of life, there is a wound that comes with it.

Believing and experiencing ourselves as separate from creation and the creator, that we are alone in the world in our perceived uniqueness, can be immensely painful. We strive to "get ahead," we fight, struggle to be right, or to be loved. What rang true for me with this idea was seeing how people continue to try to identify a reason for the primal wound of being human. They go to therapy, explore the effects of abusive parents, try the latest self-help fad, all based on the belief that the wound of being human is wrong, that it was inflicted on us in this life or a past one, and can be cured with the right healer, pill, or therapy.

In relationships, we have the opportunity to experience the veil of separation differently. In an enjoyable relationship experience, especially when we first connect and fall in love, the feeling of togetherness, connection, and intimacy allow us to feel what it is like to be so deeply connected to another that we can don't experience so much aloneness. We tap into that divine experience that transcends the physical, and get a glimpse through the veils. Our lovers can show us what it is like to hold another so much in our hearts that we place their interest equal with our own, that we cannot win if it means they lose.

Even as the first divine flush of love fades, a close romantic relationship can provide much distraction from the deep sense of aloneness we feel by being in human form. With someone to share meals and activities, we may not meet that empty space inside ourselves as strongly. Perhaps the relationship is difficult and hard. If the goal is to avoid meeting yourself, a tumultuous, unhappy relationship serves very well as a distraction.

One of the primary things that is so painful about a relationship ending is that it brings us forcefully face to face with the primal wound, the suffering caused by being in an experience that requires the illusion of separation. We are often depleted when we get there, for a relationship going downhill often wears us out and bruises our hearts. I know I have lingered overly long in relationships that weren't working in the hopes of avoiding the pain or to avoid inflicting the pain of a break up.

## Letting go and trusting

In addition, when there is something that partially meets my needs, it is harder to let it go. The known quantity gets comfortable; I rationalize and weigh the "pluses" and the "minuses." Looking over my life, I can see themes of holding onto lovers, jobs, living spaces, and activities that were once fulfilling long after they had stopped bringing me the joy and value that they once held for me.

It seems like the realization of "Hey, I'm not having fun anymore. This really isn't making me happy," would make it easy move on. I know people who have that gift and clarity and fundamental trust in the universe that allows them to release the things that no longer serve without struggle. But most of us cling. Many are familiar with the idea of scarcity as it pertains to money—no matter how much we have, it never seems like enough. Yet we also cling to unhappy relationships with partners, jobs, hobbies, and friends with this idea that something is better than nothing.

It takes great courage and trust in the universe to step away from a job, a relationship, a hobby, even a habit or way of being in the world. It is hard to give up the warm place of that which is known, predictable and familiar, even if it is warm shit. Believing that we will not get the things we truly want gives us a level of permission not to open fully, not to give our best, to keep protecting our hearts.

Relationships to lovers are an especially powerful place to see this clinging. In my journeys for clients, I often see how a painful situation depletes the person so that their ability to manifest, grow, and seek something better is diminished. People stay because they look inside and find themselves so depleted that the steps to leave and build a new life seem exhausting, too much to handle, until things become unbearably miserable. What they don't see is how when their energy isn't tied up with the perpetual motion misery machine of a bad relationship, they will have so much more within them to face the world.

In the physical world, we, as small children, worked out our understanding that two objects can't occupy the same space at the same time. We tried to put two blocks or toys in the same space, hit them together, trying to make them fit, then repeated this process many more times. Eventually we learned and accepted that in order to have a thing fit in a given spot, we must move whatever is already there to create an empty space that allows the new object to be placed there.

But somehow as we grow up that time of empty space becomes frightening. Perhaps it is partly because we meet ourselves, all the dark, painful, lost, scared parts, when we are alone after something ends. Yet, I've often found that after all the dreading and resisting the end of a relationship, after a storm of tears, the predominant emotion is great relief.

## Resisting intimacy and relationships

As much as people resist walking away from relationships, they can resist getting into them with equal determination. I work with many clients whose chief complaint is their inability to find a romantic partner.

I've come to realize how much the human fear of change plays into the forming and leaving of relationship. When a person is single, for all that a part of them longs for an intimate relationship, other parts remember the last relationship and all the bad times. Often, in order to keep the peace in a relationship, one partner or the other with swallow their truth and/or allow themselves to be treated in unkind and disrespectful ways. The vulnerable part of the self that is disregarded in this situation may feel like being single is a way to be safe. Sometimes the emotional risk of getting close to someone who may disappoint you feels too great.

I've certainly had moments of knowing that I needed to heal before I would be able to risk my heart in romantic love again. Knowledge that I wasn't ready, however, has not prevented me from struggling with the desire to fill the empty place with the next decorative, interesting person. After all, I am perfectly capable of manifesting the exact relationship that will teach me the lesson that I'm still working on. So, if there is one part of you that doesn't want a relationship and one that does, you broadcast two conflicting signals to the universe with equal strength: bring me a love, don't bring me a love. The universe may conclude that you have not yet learned that you are broadcasting conflicting signals and sends you an opportunity to learn clarity in what you ask for or your life may remain in a holding pattern until you are sending a clear signal

As a person goes through life and grows and heals and learns, they manifest better and better experiences. So whether walking away from a relationship that doesn't serve or an experience of being single, change often means giving up the best thing we've had so far and stepping into unknown territory. All our fears arise, all our unhealed wounds from the past get stirred up, and we question ourselves and look for excuses to retreat back to what is familiar, whether it is running away from the smallest flaw in a new person who has caught our eye or reasoning our way out of our truth about how broken our current relationship may be.

## Come back to yourself

The lesson I come back to, again and again, is our relationship to ourselves is at the core. If we build deep trust with our inner self, especially the inner child part, this act of courage in embracing change becomes easier. All too often we treat ourselves as we were treated as children, silencing and punishing the part of ourselves that speaks an inconvenient truth.

I found that in walking away from the relationship I mentioned at the beginning of the chapter, I made it harder for myself by rejecting and making wrong the part of me that still loved the other person and wanted to be with him. It made sense why I did it. I had come to a place of knowing that this relationship didn't serve me, that I was not going to get my needs met by someone who didn't have the ability to meet his own needs at that time, let alone anyone else's. So, I wanted to not love him, long for him, or send energetic cords to reconnect our hearts. Knowing that my course of action was clear, I wanted all the parts of myself on board, working together to walk away.

The trouble with this was the more I criticized and got angry at the parts of myself that still wanted him, the more I reinforced the reason that I had been with him in the first place. He had made me feel loved. The more my heart hurt, the more deeply I longed to feel that love. If I didn't give it to myself, the more inclined I was to want to dive back into the fantasy of the relationship, and the harder some part of me would try to hold on.

In this process, I confirmed for myself once again that try as I might to overcome feeling with logic, there are simply parts of my being that don't care about logic at all. Self-love and compassion were the only things that helped my heart through that time. In fact, I ultimately came to realize that the part of me that didn't want the pain of loving this man any more was also the part of me that wanted to get rid of my vulnerable, emotional self because it kept feeling things that I didn't want to experience. Both the external relationship and my internal landscape were metaphors for how I struggled to be in control.

Ideally, at all times, especially times of relationship change, it is possible to be loving and compassionate and make space for each part of ourselves—the part that longs to return to or stay in a relationship that doesn't serve—or the part that fights against opening our heart and life to some new person. And, it is equally important to hold with love and compassion the part of ourselves that wants to silence and suppress the aforementioned part. I find it useful to have a dialog with myself and acknowledge the efforts and feelings of all levels of my being, then take the action that feels right. I don't let my inner child run the show, but I strive to make space for her to have her feelings and her say.

## What do you want?
I love being in a relationship. I love having company and companionship, someone to eat with and to tell about my day. There is

a part of myself that is capable of such deep love and devotion and thrives in having space to express that. It feels cozy and safe and wonderful to connect deeply with a lover and a partner, to envision and dream a future and a life together.

It is equally true that I love being single. It is great not to worry about someone else's needs, and I like sleeping alone–sex is great, but it is nice to have the bed to myself when I'm sleeping. I enjoy being able to plan my time and energy based on what I want. I love the feeling that I'm totally able to flirt with and play with the potential of love with everyone I meet; it adds a feeling of excitement each time I meet a new, attractive person. My relationships with friends and other people in my life get deeper when I don't have a partner, and casual, loving sexual relationships can be wonderful for me.

## What is your pattern?

What I dislike and struggle with is the change between being in a relationship and being single, in either direction. If I'm single and someone touches my heart, my head is off to the races. Sometimes before the first date has even happened, I'm begging my guides to tell me if we'll marry and grow old together. I become hyper-focused on whether and when he'll call, whether my discernment is correct, can I trust him, what about sex, what does he think of me? These questions and thoughts fly through my head; I get wound up on adrenaline and stressed. I want a crystal ball that will tell me whether this person is good for me now and always, so that if I do go into a relationship with them, I won't ever get my heart broken. As you can see quite a bit of fear gets stirred up!

I also loathe leaving relationships. There is always such a struggle between the conflicted parts of myself–some that say leave, others that say stay. Getting clear on that is exhausting. When I leave a partner that I love deeply, there is a time when I feel like everything in my life is gray and meaningless. I'm tired, sad, and alone. The intensity of my emotions stirs up some of my most primal fears and I become terrified. I often find that once I leave, while it is bad for a while, it is seldom as bad as I have imagined. There is a trade-off for when I leave—the sooner I walk out the door, the more love, good wishes and desire for the other person remain, so the grief is sharper and the tendency to doubt my choice is more apparent. The later I leave, the less there is to mourn about the person, but I am more depleted from the pain that has gone before, leading me to the point where leaving is a clear and obvious choice. While the grieving for the person is almost over in the second case, the length of time I've spent being tired and worn out lasts much longer.

## Discernment

When is it good to work on it (the relationship) and when is it good to walk away? Amid all these conflicting voices–those that say go and those that say stay–it is hard to hear myself think. I have great stamina for a) fighting change, and b) working on myself, to make it work with someone I love. This doesn't always serve me.

I tend to seek outside help in the form of therapy in my relationship struggles. Whether the relationship ultimately ends or not, it is the journey that is important. I didn't have many models of happy relationships when I was growing up, so getting some help with skills allows me to struggle and flail less. Whether I stay or go, if I'm working on myself, I grow. There are levels of healing that cannot be accessed outside a romantic relationship because nothing else so effectively triggers those deep vulnerabilities and wounds.

There are still relationships that are helpful and valuable even through the struggle. My guides always say it just comes down to choice. There are things to be learned going or staying, both choices are just different ways to engage with a life lesson. As long as abuse and harm are not occurring, there is no right or wrong answer. My most unpleasant relationship coincided with a time of immense growth. And, ultimately, not being with that person made my life much happier and richer, despite the depth of the love I had felt.

Some of my dearest friends have given me the amazing gift of supporting me in through times in relationships where I'm experiencing suffering. It is hard and painful to watch someone you love stay with someone who doesn't honor them, love them, and make them happy in the way that you know they deserve to be. It is a tremendous gift to hold space for their struggle in a way that allows them to stay or go and know that they are supported. Sometimes it is not possible. I remember telling one friend that I loved her, but I couldn't hold space for her to go around and around with this man any more. She was exceptional enough to be able to hear this, honor it, and have it deepen our connection, rather than damage it.

## Anger

In my work, I get to see people take emotional roads to extreme places. Like the man who believed he was cursed because everything kept going wrong over a three-year period. Actually he was deeply, deeply angry. He never allowed himself to experience the pain of a betrayal he survived, so he stayed stuck in the anger—and living in anger generates problems in relationships, health, money, etc. It was a vicious cycle as all the consequence that being angry created just made him angrier, while providing fuel for his story that those who wronged him three years ago were to blame for his current suffering.

Anger is an effective, if ultimately damaging, way to avoid pain. On the emotional scale, anger is a step up from sadness, depression, and pain. It is closer to the top of the scale, which is crowned with joy and happiness. Although we need to fully experience all the emotions, unfortunately people sometimes get as far as anger and stop there to avoid pain, which is so much more uncomfortable. We all have our shadow emotions. There are those who can't experience anger or are afraid of it, and those who are angry all the time to avoid feeling pain and sadness.

In a breakup, there is always a part of me that is angry. I may tell myself the story that the other person has failed me in some way or blame them for the deep pain. If I feel rejected, I am angry at them for not valuing me enough. If I am the one leaving, I feel angry that they failed to listen and change when I tried so hard to find a way to work out our differences. There is the good part of the anger, the part that finally allows me to acknowledge fully all the ways that I wasn't valued, heard, acknowledged, and cherished. This is often an experience that I have been suppressing, because if I fully connect with it and experience it, I will no longer be willing to tolerate being in that relationship under those circumstances. To allow myself to feel anger before I'm ready to leave means to risk the relationship that some part of me is still fighting to hold onto.

At that point it is easy for some of my least attractive shadow parts to arise. Out of this anger and hurt, I could find myself wanting to hurt the other person, to lash out. I believe strongly in the principle of honoring the love of a relationship by leaving as kindly and gently as possible. For all that it feels like the end of everything, I know that once I have passed grief and have moved on, the warm feelings I felt for the person will likely outweigh the pain, unless bad behavior on one side or the other has overshadowed the memory of the love. My relationship exit strategy, therefore, is always along the high road, but even as I walk this road, I am sometimes keenly aware of the unattractive desire to punish the other person.

## Pain

Because breakups are so hard, sometime it feels easier to go back rather than move through the pain. We may wait until things are so bad and so painful that there is very little to lose by walking away.

The Kübler-Ross model establishes the five stages of grieving: Denial, Anger, Bargaining, Depression, and Acceptance. For me, those stages don't happen in a nice, linear fashion when I break up with someone. Instead, they tend to jumble together as I bounce from one feeling to another. At the core of the parting of ways is profound pain. There are tears and a deep ache in my heart, and if it is really bad, my whole body can ache. Often the process of fighting and reaching the truth causes some amount of intestinal upset, leaving me nauseous and crampy. My heart physically hurts and there is a gigantic weight in the pit of my stomach. The emotion feels huge.

I sit with this as long as I can manage, breathing into to it, allowing it just to be. I try not to struggle against it, to wind myself up with distress that I am so distressed. At some point, I reach my limit for being with what I'm feeling and switch into something else to avoid the grief.

Perhaps I fantasize about the other person rushing to the rescue. If I've been left, I sit in the feeling of rejection and imagine them rushing after me, telling me how they are a fool, that I'm the best thing that ever happened to them, promising that everything will be different. I imagine some great change and realization on their part that leads them to being the good partner that I've experienced as their unrealized potential. In this I must remind myself to come back to myself. Despite my detailed and (in my opinion) entirely accurate knowledge of their flaws and what therapeutic steps and interpersonal work would fix them, sharing that information is unhelpful. If they wanted to work on these things, they would have, and to point out their flaws in the perfect, most accurate, and clearly communicated words is not going to effect change.

I spent years and years believing that if I could just find the right words to state my needs and feelings and why they were right, that the person, who said that they loved me, would promptly change. For example, if I told my partner that I had a hard time when they drank, that I didn't enjoy them under the influence, they would stop. If I asked them clearly not to publicly ask my permission in front of all our friends to have just one drink and explained how that felt when they did it, they would stop doing that as well as turning the one drink into five. I learned that all my wonderful words and being right are not something that changes people. Then I learned it again, and again, and I still test it out from time to time to see if it is still true.

This idea that I could just talk to the person and something could be said that would change all that had gone before is my bargaining and denial part of the grief process. When the feeling of the pain becomes too much to meet head on, I side step into playing with words that will make them be different.

## The rewards
Some of our scariest, most painful moments come to us with our relationships, so much so that some people choose to avoid romantic relationships all together. The pain of loss, disappointed hopes and the way we are brought face to face with some of our deepest fears can be hard to endure. The struggle for clarity about when to go and when to stay, about what's your issue and what's the other person's, can be confusing and exhausting.

Understanding the intensity of this pain can help us to cultivate compassion for those who engage in apparently self-destructive behaviors such as alcohol or drug use or creating a "relationship back-up plan" with infidelity. Even more importantly, sitting with the pain is a place to cultivate deep compassion for yourself. My experience is that by being present with and allowing myself to feel the ouchy stuff, I create a deep well of personal strength and stamina, as well as the flexibility to flow with change.

# Chapter 13—The Shamanic Perspective

Shamanism is not a religion; rather it is a worldview or perspective. I often describe it as a framework for understanding the unseen world. We are energetic and spiritual beings as much as we are physical. Shamanism provides a framework for understanding the non-physical aspects of our being and how they connect to the greater universe.

The shamanic perspective can be challenging to accept because it operates from some premises that are outside mainstream Western thought. Shamanism provides a way of understanding some part of the cosmos that we can't see or touch directly. While the notion of interacting with spiritual guides may seem far-fetched in our modern, scientific age, the practice has arisen independently in indigenous cultures throughout the world. The actual tools and techniques of shamanism are straightforward, relatively simple, and very thoroughly tested.

One of these premises is that all things have spirit— —the rocks, the clouds, the trees, the earth itself. Furthermore, it is possible to interact with these spirits. Shamanic journeying is a method used in many cultures to send personal awareness into the symbolic, non-rational realm of myth and dreams. Mind-traveling is a traditional means of interacting with spiritual guides and allies for guidance and personal healing.

I see the universe as the ideal parent, without all the human limitations and lessons to trip over. Many indigenous cultures hold that the earth and sky are our true parents; the people we call mom and dad are merely temporary guardians.

Within this relationship, our guides and the universe itself desire our happiness. They will not support us in having things that are harmful to us. A dear friend of mine tried to talk her father into giving her a weather balloon for her eighth birthday. She thought flying would be fun. Her dad said no, but offered her a pony. Our spiritual parents fulfill our requests in a similar fashion.

When we choose to incarnate on earth, we set up goals and contracts and life lessons. We make our plans, pick our parents, and are born into physical form. Once we are in physical form, we have no way of knowing what those lessons, contracts, and goals were, unless we learn to access them through some kind of psychic practice, such as shamanic journey. Even then, we only get glimpse, rather than the full picture. As we walk through life, our guides, who have access to all this information, work to support us in the life path we have chosen. They put the right people in our path to support us, they help keep us safe, they whisper in our dream and intuition about which choices will serve us best.

As some point, we are often faced with the question: If we are loved, how can bad things happen to good people? If the universe and our guides are looking over us, how can horrible things like molest, rape, and torture happen?

My experience of the answer is that these bad things are connected to the lessons we have chosen to learn. On a soul level, we have this brief moment of time when we wear these veils and think that the human experience is all that there is. On a soul level, the worst events of our lives may be as minor as falling down and bruising ourselves when we were learning to walk. We often learn lessons by experiencing the positive and negative aspects of the energy, the lesson of grace by experiencing both the presence of it and the lack of it in our lives, for example.

## Past life connections

Many times we are the ones making life harder than it needs to be. For example, I had a client who grew up with a neglectful and extremely abusive mother. There was sexual abuse from mom's boyfriend and it caused a great deal of soul trauma. When I worked with my client, my guides said that in order to understand this woman's choice to be born to a damaged and mentally ill mother, I needed to see her most recent past life.

In this past life, my client was a man, a prison guard who abused his power. The woman who became my client's mother in this lifetime was a woman who was imprisoned. The guard raped, beat, and abused his prisoner until she died. Later in his life, the prison guard evolved as a person and had tremendous, overwhelming remorse for what he had done. The guilt and the pain of the abuse he had inflicted overwhelmed him. The force of his feeling that he deserved to be punished created the contract and intent to incarnate and be the victim as a way to atone and allow his soul to release the guilt.

So, when I did healing for my client, it was necessary to heal the guilt and pain of the past life as well as the abuse and trauma from this lifetime. There wasn't an external need for punishment, but it was something that the soul created.

The law of karma across various traditions states the effects of all one's deeds actively create past, present, and future experiences, thus making one responsible for one's own life, and the pain and joy it brings to oneself and others. It's not about retribution, but about consequences. These consequences extend beyond the present lifetime and the current choices. In the case of my client, the consequence was a compelling need to come to terms with past actions and find self-forgiveness. The route her soul picked was incarnating into an abusive situation.

The law of attraction reflects the larger experience of karma. Because the law of attraction functions locally, within this lifetime, and often within the hour or day, it can be easier to understand. According to the law of attraction, whatever we put out into the world comes back to us.

If we are in alignment in our lives, the world around us aligns with us. If we are rude to people, we attract unpleasant, rude people. If we cheat others, we expect to be cheated and create that experience. There's a great elegance to this approach because it allows people to simply engage with other people working with the same type of energy they are experiencing. The universe doesn't punish us for bad behavior; we instead dance the victim/perpetrator relationship with other souls that are working on the same lessons.

## How like attracts like

When I was working with the lesson of trying to buy approval and attention by pleasing and over-giving to others, I attracted people who were very good at using others. My first Reiki master was a great example of this. I perceived her as very powerful and connected to spirit. I wanted to be special to her, to have her attention, to have her connect me to spirit. She was most delighted to live rent free in my house. She also believed she was important, special, and should be exempt from paying her way or doing housework. Owning that I chose this lesson, rather than blaming her for taking advantage of me, allowed me to keep my power. While it wasn't fun, this insight allows me to make different choices when presented with the same or similar situation. It also helps me clarify my boundaries about rescuing people and bringing wounded people home with me.

The mistake I believe people make about karma or law of attraction is assuming that it is a balancing of the scales. Somehow there's this idea of a universal score keeper who makes sure we get rewarded for goodness and punished for our sins. My experience is that we create our own reality. If we believe we will and must be punished, we attract that experience. However, at the point we learn the lesson and choose again, we can simply step away from the energy of the experience, whether we're on the victim or perpetrator part of the cycle. Sometimes the energy from our former choices is still in motion and plays out before aligning to our new choices, and we can realize this as the linear consequences of our actions, or as punishment.

For instance, let's say you punch someone in the nose when they say something you don't like. You then realize that this was a poor choice, forgive yourself and the other person, and then come to a place where you can honor your desire to punch others in the nose without acting on it. Once you have fully integrated the lesson that led to the loss of control and the nose punch, by law of attraction, you will no longer draw people and situations to you that involve nose punching. However, the energy that you have put into motion when you punched the other person is still in motion. You may get punched right back! You may have to deal with the legal ramifications of your choice. It's not retribution when the other person smacks you, just energy still in motion.

In the example of my client whose mother was so abusive, there was nothing in the universe that required my client to incarnate and experience being a victim to make up for having abused another as a prison guard. However, while the soul grew to the point in the prison guard lifetime to understand and truly integrate a knowing that abuse was wrong, he was not able to grasp and master the lessons of forgiveness and compassion for self. So, my client set up a lifetime to complete those lessons, since it is often easier to forgive another than ourselves. Furthermore, it was how the soul chose to release the guilt and pain at having been the abuser. If there had been self-forgiveness in the former lifetime, the soul would likely not have selected an abusive mother.

## And so shamanic practice!
This is part of why I'm so passionate about doing shadow work and embracing all aspects of the self. If we can look at our dark parts, find our inner abuser, our hidden murderer, the part of us that flows hatred, and still hold ourselves in love and grace, we can stop creating so much suffering for ourselves and in the world. We don't need to reject others for the sin of mirroring back a part of ourselves we don't want to look at. By giving attention to all aspects of our beings we cease wasting energy fighting to suppress and ignore "undesirable" parts of ourselves. If we can love ourselves, we don't need to wear masks in the

world to prevent others from seeing that which we wish to hide from our own awareness.

Another aspect of the life experience is what happens when we go through trauma and suffering. While it may allow us to activate and complete life lessons, sometimes it also diminishes our life force energy. When we experience soul loss due to trauma, we find our energy and vitality reduced, a state of diminishment that can make us vulnerable to illness as well as those looking to victimize. The necessity for spiritual as well as physical healing following trauma explains why some form of soul retrieval work is found in indigenous cultures throughout the world.

I've also worked with people who have been so wounded that they have disconnected themselves from the universe. In a process of denying God, renouncing the divine, or closing out the universe, they have become disconnected from the flow of universal source energy. With these people, I often get a strong, urgent tap on the shoulder from their guides to help correct the situation so that other layers of healing can follow.

## Destiny path energy
Our energy, our choices create energy flow. This concept makes a great deal of sense to me as an engineer. Obtaining my engineering degree required a thorough study of physics. I learned about inertia, the concept that an object in motion tends to remain in motion unless and until some other force acts upon it. For example, if you throw a ball, it keeps going until the force of wind resistance and gravity or hitting a wall makes it stop.

Our destiny energy demonstrates similar principles. Our choices, our past lives, our contracts, whatever we're thinking and feeling in the moment, create a river of energy flowing toward a given outcome. I believe good psychics aren't telling the future; they're tuning into the momentum of your choices. If you keep making the same choices, a given outcome is very likely, such as focusing your energy towards a degree earns you the degree. Or, if you keep using your energy to control others and aren't honest with yourself about your motivations, you will eventually become ill and/or have difficult relationships.

The difficulty of changing the path of your destiny energy is proportional to the momentum you've accumulated. Each choice you make down that path incurs momentum. Think of trying to stop a ball thrown gently towards you versus one hit with a bat. The energetic accrual of a thousand choices ultimately contributes to whether some illnesses are terminal and some are not. There are people who learn deeply important lessons on their death bed and die with a sense of completing their life lessons with success, mastering them only in the last days of their life.

To recover completely from a life threatening illness requires tremendous transformation in a dramatically short time to truly anchor the energy of life and health in opposition to illness. My terminally ill clients often ask, "How can I live? What will heal me?" I can do much to ease their circumstance, but the message the guides have always delivered in these cases is the overriding need for a deep, passionate life wish. A passionate fear of dying is not the same as a life wish. To long to see the seasons change, or find out what's around the corner, to hold the will and desire to live and thrive while in chronic pain or depletion is challenging.

One of the joys of Western medicine is that we can reduce physical suffering, which makes it easier to embrace one's life wish. Western medicine buys us time to complete the lessons, opening more choices for our destiny. It allows terminal illnesses to become a final warning to change our path if we want to live, rather than the beginning of the end.

## Watch out for that turn
I like Alberto Villoldo's description of what happens when you change a destiny path overnight. He compares it to driving down the freeway at 60 miles per hour in a loaded pickup truck. Suddenly, without slowing down, you make a right turn. You slide, screech and skid through the turn, and you make it, but the baggage that you had in the

back of the pickup doesn't make the turn with you. Be aware of the fact it will fly out and fall in the road.

This is part of why I have my clients read an article before their session that talks about how your life can change with shamanic healing. The work that I do vastly accelerates my client's ability to grow and heal and create a joyful life. It can be a sudden step into a higher vibration, especially if they follow the suggestions of their guides. But it is also a big life change. I love being able to transform my life for the better overnight, but there's a price. People, activities, ideas of who I am and physical attachments all get swept away, creating space for that which is in my new highest and best. I wouldn't change my choices. It seems like every month that goes by, my life gets richer, fuller, and more satisfying to my soul. But the two-month period in which I moved twice, left my romantic relationship, and resigned from my engineering job pushed me to find new levels of strength I didn't know I had and preferred not to need.

The universe brings us our lessons in the gentlest possible way that still gets our attention, be it a tap on the shoulder or a boot to the head. In the case of all the aforementioned life changes in a short time, I was in resistance to changing certain things, even though those things were no longer serving my best interests.

**In regard to moving:** I had known for a year that the place I lived no longer served me, and I wanted to move. I let my fears of the process override my desire for a new place. In my romantic relationship, I had been fighting the lessons before me, trying to simultaneously hold onto old ways and get new results. When I finally chose to give up the old ways and commit fully to the relationship, I received the clarity that I needed that this wasn't a relationship that would honor my most joyful path. Remaining in it would be like wearing a shoe two sizes too small. I needed to give up my old patterns of hiding, manipulating, and people-pleasing to be present in my truth before I could have clarity.

**As for my engineering job:** I had been fighting with myself over working there for the better part of a year. I was scared to step away from the security of a regular paycheck and the accomplishment of being a woman in a primarily male profession, so I forced myself to keep that job, and I struggled every day to make myself go, to make myself perform the work. Still employed, I went to Hawaii after my relationship ended where I experienced a profound rebirth in a sacred yoni cave. As I sat, deep under the earth, in the womb of Pele, I answered the question of whether I was ready to release the old to allow in the new with a deep "yes." I invited the universe to clear away the things that no longer served. I suspect the change with my engineering job happened almost the moment I told the universe of my intent as I made the change shortly after returning from that trip.

Everything associated with leaving my engineering job happened in the gentlest possible way. My employers gave me the choice to go back to full time or be laid off. I knew that I couldn't go back from 18 hours a week to 40, everything in me said no, but at least I had a choice. It made my leaving as gentle and clear a choice as possible.

**With my home:** When my romantic relationship ended, my partner was angry and hurt and I needed to move at once. I remember lying awake in bed after I'd said I was leaving and telling my guides that by the end of the next day, I needed to know where I was living. I needed them to manifest a wonderful place for me and to make it very, very clear, because I was not at my intuitive best. I needed it to be easy. I had a new place by 4 p.m. the next day—and I absolutely loved my new home.

I also got to see how supported I was. I had friends calling the whole time I went through the breakup. My friends dropped everything to help me move. I felt utterly supported in all the changes I experienced in that tumultuous couple of months.

The resistance generated by my fear of change established a web of tension between all the good intentions and choices I was visioning for myself, like growing my business and working on my personal growth. My fears had me staying in a job that I didn't want, a home that didn't nurture me, and a one-foot-in-one-foot-out romantic relationship. So, when I released my resistance and struggle against change that was in my highest and best interests, the destiny path energy shifted all too quickly; like a rubber band where the energetic potential had been stretched to the breaking point and then released. It was hard on my human self that craves security and stability. And, it was totally worth it.

## Interpersonal transmutation

Not all suffering is the result of some lesson, vulnerability created by something unhealed, or a failure to listen about a change. Sometimes it is merely a powerful opportunity. For example, I worked with a woman whose son had died. His death provided an opportunity for her to come into a destiny as a healer through the Mother Mary archetype, experiencing a transpersonal healing of grace through loss and suffering, being able to witness the pain of others with compassion and love and without flinching away. When people grow and heal through difficult events, their transformation contributes to the collective consciousness and others can more easily find relief and healing from their own similar suffering. On a shamanic level, the idea of embracing suffering (since you're going through it anyway) with the intent that others may be free of it, has a great deal of power.

# Chapter 14—Shamanic Healing of Sexuality

This chapter specifically addresses the shamanic and energetic aspects of healing. Throughout the book, there are many different ways and means of healing and opening to this important aspect of yourself— — your sexuality. Taking any of these suggestions and working with them will put healing into motion on all levels. In fact, just reading this book can be a significant step leading to healing. Using healing techniques in multiple areas will put the healing into motion much faster.

My kissing quest and other sexual exploration provided real world, day to day healing and opening of my sexuality. As personal wounds and self-imposed limitations were revealed to me, applying my shamanic talents gave me the opportunity to vastly accelerate the healing process by addressing the energetic/spiritual aspects of the damage.

## Reiki treatments

My spiritual and shamanic path began with Reiki. The term Reiki refers both to universal healing energy as well as the system used to channel it. A quick primer: every living thing is imbued with life force energy recognized by many names across the world, such as "chi" in China, "mana" to the Hindu and "ki" in Japan. It is the life force energy responsible for the "life" of our physical bodies. For us to not just live but to thrive, this life force energy must flow freely through our bodies without blockages and be in abundant supply.

Energetically sensitive people often experience profound relief and healing from Reiki treatments. For me, working with Reiki techniques allowed me to begin to move energy that was stagnant in my body. Old emotions, pain, and patterns began to clear and my personal healing journey gained momentum the more I used Reiki.

Reiki practitioners and teachers abound. A basic level one attunement to Reiki will allow you to channel this wonderful energy for yourself and others. In selecting a Reiki practitioner for individual sessions or a Reiki teacher, listen closely to your intuition. Unlike massage and other holistic healing practices, Reiki is unregulated, so there's a lot of variation within the community. At the core, Reiki is a very simple practice, so I rely on my intuition regarding the person's clarity and openness as well as whether they are embracing or rejecting their shadow when selecting an energy worker. I recommend avoiding Reiki classes that teach all three levels in a weekend. I've found it works better to space out the different levels.

## Additional treatment options

As I've stated in previous chapters, the damage caused by sexual trauma affects the individual on many levels. On a social or interpersonal level, sexually charged situations and experiences can feel dangerous or overwhelming, making it a struggle to define and hold boundaries and to feel safe in the world. The physical body may be imprinted with the energy of trauma, trapped as a "body memory", which can lead to disease and illness, especially in the area of the sexual and reproductive organs. On the spiritual level, sexual trauma causes soul loss and negatively impacts the energetic body.

It may sound a bit overwhelming, but actually this pervasive wounding is all interconnected. Therefore, any of these areas can be worked on directly. The healing of one area impacts all the others and can activate a spontaneous healing. For example, moving stagnant energy in the belly through dance or Qi Gong (usually pronounce *cheh kongh*) can lead to naturally feeling less fear in a sexual situation or having less painful periods. Kissing men and getting comfortable with sexual energy can cause energetic structures to clear away on their own, now that the fear that held them in place has been alleviated. Individual or group therapy can activate deep healing. Just getting a massage can promote great healing of post-traumatic stress, according to some studies.

## Soul retrieval

One of the most powerful techniques for sexual healing is soul retrieval. It can be done in an hour and creates a fundamental transformation in your life. I'd been working with Reiki and a number of other healing modalities for a few years before I experienced soul retrieval. After receiving my own soul retrieval, I realized that if I only got to do one thing for a client, I wanted it to be this—it is a powerful, penetrating, and often life changing healing. Unlike Reiki, in which the client can shift back into familiar energetic patterns following a treatment, soul retrieval makes a fundamental change to the client's energy structure. For someone who has done a significant amount of personal work, it can be the final piece. For someone just beginning a healing path, it can add a source of strength and wholeness right from the beginning, as an anchor point for healing.

The soul, as referred to in soul retrieval, is the energetic essence of your being. It encompasses the intangible aspects of your being, including gifts, qualities, and aspects of who you are. It is the "you" that transcends physical experience. Pieces and parts of that soul essence can sometimes become separated, trapped, and/or lost. If you imagine the soul energy as a sphere, when soul loss occurs, there are voids and areas that are missing, leaving empty spaces in that structure.

## How we lose soul pieces

Soul loss is designed to protect our nonphysical essence from various kinds of trauma. During a traumatic experience such as car accident, sexual violence, or an emotional assault, the last place we want to be is fully present in our bodies, aware of what is happening. Instead, part of us goes away to avoid the trauma and to attempt to preserve the original integrity or purity of the consciousness. Psychologists refer to this as dissociation. The shamanic community calls it soul loss.

Whatever the trauma, the protective mechanism of soul loss causes part of our life essence to leave in order to protect itself from being damaged or traumatized. The soul part that leaves sometimes carries away some of the memory and immediacy of the experience. In the normal course of events, the soul part would return on its own after the trauma had passed. But sometimes, as in the case of molest or sexual violence, the trauma is so severe that the soul part goes so far and fast that it can't find its way back and gets lost. In cases of chronic trauma or abuse, the soul part may not know it is safe to come back. There's no time in shamanic reality, so the soul part doesn't know that twenty years have passed and the violent stepfather is no longer in the picture.

Whatever the source of soul loss, the effects are much the same. Soul loss will diminish a person's sense of well-being and joy in life, and it can cause a lack of vitality and interest in the world. People missing soul parts often feel depressed and listless, and as though the world was all gray. Soul loss can lead to gaps in memory; people can feel fragmented or spacey or even as though pieces of themselves are missing. Sometimes people become accident-prone or keep falling into the path of misfortune. People with soul loss can spend a lot of energy working through events of their past and still feel impacted by them. In extreme cases, soul loss can cause a lack of sense of self, suicidal tendencies, and vulnerability to physical illness.

When I do a soul retrieval for a client, I shift my awareness into a light trance state. I can then find and return the pieces of a person's essence that have become separated. It can be done in about an hour, in person, over the phone, or even via email. Some conventional therapists are beginning to refer their clients for soul retrieval work as part of the healing process.

If you've experienced molest, rape, physical or emotional abuse, I highly recommend getting a soul retrieval, and having it done for you, not as a self-help project. Soul retrieval is one of the few healing practices that I would not recommend trying to do for yourself without the help of a trained facilitator. Some people get spontaneous soul return, where other healing causes pieces to return on their own.

Nevertheless, getting some help, whether from me or another practitioner, is one of the fastest and most efficient ways to heal from sexual trauma.

## Soul retrieval for healing sexuality

When someone comes to me with sexual trauma, in addition to the soul retrieval work, I apply my special "Shamanic Healing for Sexual Trauma" approach as part of the session.

One common side effect of sexual trauma is that the lower chakras can get shut down. Sometimes survivors of sexual trauma become very sexual later on, and in that case, they don't usually have as much of a problem. The victims who do shut down their sexuality tend to close the lower half of their energy body, which includes the solar plexus chakra, the power and will center. The solar plexus chakra is the center of psychic intuition and sense of self. If you tune in to how a choice or experience feels in the area of this chakra, you can connect with your deepest truth. Having this chakra closed makes it more difficult to stand up for yourself, take action, and hold boundaries.

The sacral chakra is our sexual center, a great source of vitality, life force energy, creative energy and power. Having this chakra closed down makes the world seem gray and dull. It is pretty much impossible to be in our passion without this center being activated.

The root chakra is our connection to mother earth. Having this chakra open and flowing allows us to be energetically fed by earth energy, stay grounded and present in our bodies and participate fully in the physical world. When the root chakra is closed, we get spacey, tired, and are more likely to dissociate.

So, when I'm working with someone who has had sexual trauma, I begin working with their energy bodies to open up these three chakras, to create strong and healthy roots into the earth, and to clear away the energy of trauma. This is something that can be done on your own. See Chapter 19 for techniques and exercises to open up the chakras and clear out the stagnant energy.

The next thing I do is to work directly on the sexual trauma. With sexual trauma, the wounding is so intense that memory and intensity of the experience creates an imprint somewhere in shamanic reality. The thoughts, pain, and memory (whether processed on a conscious or unconscious level) create a strong energetic cord to that experience. It leaves my clients with an energetic door open to their trauma all the time. Most of the time, this energy exchange is white noise in their energy field. But moments like feeling sexual energy can wake up and activate the energy of the trauma, causing fear and stress in the current moment around sexuality.

I go back to the incident and do healing work at the source. Human beings are actually designed to process trauma and pain and release it very effectively, but we don't always have the tools needed in these situations. Part of the reason that people often heal more easily and completely from trauma such as loss of a loved one or a personal disaster or illness is that the community support around such things is powerful and focused. Around sexual trauma, our society is kind of nuts, alternately blaming the victim and trying to sweep things under the rug.

In shamanic reality I can go back and provide the five year old or the twenty year old with unconditional love and support and hold space while the energy is processed and released. Once that happens, the past incident is no longer anchored in shamanic reality and the energy can dissipate and return to universal source energy. At that point, trauma and pain can be released easily from my client's current energy field. Doing inner child work, as I describe later in the book, can accomplish this part of the healing.

## Victim/Perpetrator relationships

Often there are cords and energetic connections between abuser and victim. Sometime the abuser takes a soul piece from the victim. In shamanic reality I can cut the cords, retrieve the soul piece, and un-invite the abuser to have anything further to do with my client. If the abuser has passed on, I can help them complete their ascension process and hand them back over to their guides for their own healing and karmic processing.

Sometimes the guides will give me information about why, on a soul level, my client had this kind of experience. I've learned that for some people, hearing that information is helpful in their healing process. Upon occasion a soul will incarnate where there's a higher probability of experiencing sexual abuse in order to activate and therefore release a wound of sexual trauma in another lifetime. In some cases, the soul was so eager to incarnate that they were willing to take what was available or they jumped into a bad situation, knowing that they could deal with it, even though it wouldn't be fun.

My guides have shown me how these patterns of sexual abuse go back generation after generation, as the victim becomes the perpetrator. This cycle of sexual abuse has been part of the way that people have explored the nature of power, taking turns being the one to misuse it and being the victim of its misuses. At this time, many old souls have taken on the experience of this trauma, not because they need to understand not to misuse sexuality, but in order to free the world from sexual abuses. Every time someone heals from sexual trauma, it becomes easier for others with similar trauma to heal. This healing is contributing to a universal consciousness and collective knowledge of how to release and heal sexual trauma so that it can stop being part of our world.

Sometimes a soul will take on a painful lifetime in an effort to atone and release some of the karma that has been accumulated. It is not so much that the universe demands justice or payback, but at times the soul can't bring themselves to release what they have done to others without an experience of reciprocal suffering. As humanity moves into a new phase and experience, souls are especially eager to create a clean slate to meet the new energy.

## No time in shamanic reality
All of this can be done in an hour of our real world, physical time. It is not that we can't accomplish this kind of healing by simply working

through each layer in the conscious world. However, shamanic work can powerfully accelerate the process and help people when they get stuck. Sometimes this trauma can feel so big that it is too much to just work through on our own. This was definitely the case for me. I had a lot of help and am honored to, in turn, help others along this journey. Somehow it makes what I went through totally worthwhile if I can help someone move through and heal it even faster.

Beyond the basic soul retrieval and healing of sexual trauma from this lifetime, shamanic work can allow us to go deeper into other areas and speed up the healing. If a woman is having trouble conceiving, it can be valuable to do shamanic healing around her previous lifetime experiences of motherhood. When female health issues arise, shamanic healing practices tell us to look for a deeper cause of the vulnerability. Perhaps there was a lifetime when being a woman meant abuse and trauma. Perhaps there is some resistance and pain from this lifetime about being a woman…but that is another chapter!

# Chapter 15—Masculine and Feminine Energies

When I speak of masculine and feminine energies, I'm not talking about qualities that reside exclusively in one person or another depending upon their gender. Every man or woman is a unique blend of masculine and feminine tendencies, energies, and traits. To avoid confusion, it can be easier to use the Chinese terms of yin (feminine) and yang (masculine) energy.

## Yin + yang = all of us

Yin and yang are considered to be two opposite types of energy or forces, both of which are necessary for harmony and balance. They could be described as two primal, opposing but complementary principles or cosmic forces that are found in all beings and processes in the universe.

The yin or feminine principle is about receptivity and stillness. It provides the substance and nurturing energy for all things and is often associated with the elements of earth and water. Yin energy can be considered to be dark, still, and rich. It is the realm of the unconscious and holds deep mysteries, the moon time, and timeless emotion. When in the yin energy, one is being rather than doing.

The yang or masculine energy is about action and movement, evoking the elements of fire and air. This active principle demands thinking and planning, execution of steps, working and doing rather than being. The yang-inclined person is making things happen and often uncomfortable when asked to move into a yin space of meditation and quiet.

You can apply this perception to our seasons. Summer is a yang time, working, growing, harvesting. Winter is a yin time, dreaming, resting, nurturing. Spring and fall blend the masculine and feminine energies.

In our Western culture, the yang energy or the masculine energy tends to be more valued. We tend to prize logic above emotion, action above stillness. We admire people who accomplish things and get things done, rather than those who cultivate stillness. In fact, many find their way to meditation and other forms of stillness for the sake of managing the stress of an all yang, all the time lifestyle.

## Balancing yin & yang aspects

There's an ego death in sitting in yin time, in becoming still. It is a place to meet yourself, examine who you were, who you now are, and find that you have changed. Deep truth arises in the quiet of the yin. But we are so busy, so yang. How do we dwell successfully in these two essential states of being?

Both men and women can fall into a painful imbalance between the yin and yang, the masculine and feminine. This could look like denying parts of the self that appear irrational, which is self-defeating since all of us contain within our psyches some splendid delusions. It could be about a pattern of cracking the whip on ourselves and feeling the need to achieve more and more. As an overachiever, I've had a deep fear that if I allowed myself to go into the yin state, I was being lazy and would never come out of it. Allowing myself stillness, rest and yin time remains one of my biggest challenges, along with staying with and experiencing whatever uncomfortable emotion I may be feeling.

A powerful exercise for both men and women is working to reconcile any conflict between the masculine and feminine within the self. Often we don't realize that we are at war within ourselves at the masculine/feminine level — then we wonder why we feel so tired all the time. If we work through the ways that we dishonor the masculine or feminine and come into a relationship of embracing and creating space for both, we will find more peace and well-being. Without working through our own inner conflict between these energies, it's harder to make peace between a man and a woman.

## Shamanic journey for the feminine/masculine balance

By now you probably have a good idea of whether your masculine and feminine sides are in disagreement—in fact, most of us have a level of imbalance in this area. The process of embracing and making peace between the masculine and feminine within can be done very effectively as a shamanic journey. In this journey you would go to your sacred garden (See *Practical Shamanism: A Guide for Walking in Both Worlds* for detailed instruction in shamanic journey). There you would meet with your guides and the masculine and feminine aspects of yourself.

When I did this journey, I found the masculine side of myself trying to whip the feminine into motion. The feminine responded by becoming completely immobile and unresponsive. So, I asked for power animals for each aspect. My feminine part received the butterfly, while my masculine side received a male lion. Both animals showed how they have a cyclic relationship between stillness and action. The caterpillar spins her cocoon and enters the stillness, transforms, and emerges as a butterfly, ready for great movement. The lion is still and lounges about until hunger signals the time to hunt. In hunting, it is still until it is time to attack and kill the prey.

The power animals seemed to make these aspects of myself a bit happier and I was able to talk to them. The first thing the feminine part of me said was, "Don't feel sorry for me and treat me as a victim, just because the masculine attacks me." It showed me that as long as it wasn't honored and space wasn't made, this part of me would keep her own counsel. When I chose to make space for her, she offered gifts of deep knowledge and effortless alignment of my outer life by attracting good things. She would create greater peace, abundance, and health if I allowed her time.

In the masculine, I found the parts of myself that try to control the world in order to feel safe. This part was about trying to be in action all the time. This created an imbalance and exhaustion. So, for the masculine, I looked at asking it to pull its actions back and wait until energy came to me in order to respond, rather than reaching far from myself to try to effect change. It's like moving in a martial art where the opponent's momentum is used to your advantage rather than using your own energy and directly attacking. Likewise, the masculine would be more effective adding its energy to the momentum of the universe rather than trying to create momentum out of stillness.

This exercise can also be done without shamanic journey with meditation or journaling. Write down information about the parts that are masculine and feminine. Imagine the dialogue they would have with each other: What does each part like in the other? What do they hate? How do they try to serve you? What would they wish to experience? Sit and wait for the answers to arise within you. As you uncover your relationship to the masculine and feminine within yourself, begin to look at ways to make peace with and honor both sides.

## Yin/yang manifestation techniques

When it comes to manifestation and getting things done, we can work from a yin or yang perspective. The yang or masculine way of creating outcomes is about focusing on a goal, taking aim, and achieving it through action. This could look like working hard and being goal-oriented. When it comes to ritual, this might look like gathering energy and sending it out to accomplish a goal or purpose. It is easy to understand that this is a powerful way to accomplish our goals.

Many of us are unfamiliar with the yin or feminine approach to manifestation and accomplishing goals. This approach takes advantage of the energy of desire. Instead of taking action or sending energy, the yin approach draws the desired outcome or object in. It uses the law of attraction where like attracts like, so holding the desire and a clear picture of what is desired draws that object, outcome, or experience.

## I want! The yin approach

One of the most powerful energies we can play with is the "I want" energy. This isn't the whining energy of a child, trying to get something with the feeling she might be denied, but rather the energy of pure, raw, passionate desire. It can be challenging for people, especially women, to own this energy. We are taught by frazzled parents to yield our will to theirs, to not to ask for too much. In seeking the simplest path our culture tends to shame a child for wanting too much rather than honoring the desire and setting appropriate limits.

Sometimes we need some help finding our passion. If we believe we can't expect to receive whatever we desire, we may choose to protect ourselves from pain by denying the longing exists at all. When working with the energy of desire, it's not about the future or the outcome. To use this energy effectively, simply think of what you want and imagine, as vividly as you can, how wonderful it feels to own it, to have it as a real, tangible part of your life. The joy, delight, and passion will draw it towards you. By holding that passion and delight as you imagine already having your heart's desire you will raise the resonance of the energy of desire within you, and attract more joy and good things into your life.

One advantage to the yin approach is that it requires so little output of energy and work. You are accepting and loving your inner desire and resonating out to the universe to attract fulfillment. The *Abraham-Hicks* books offer detailed instructions for this process. Instead of running around trying to make things happen (yang-style), you are inviting the energy of the universe to work on your behalf to bring you what you wish (yin-style). Success depends upon your ability to commit to deep internal work, delving within to get clear and centered about what you truly desire.

## Cleaning house

If we are looking for a romantic relationship, for example, then finding, releasing, or resolving all the parts of the self that don't want a relationship or don't believe one is possible is a good first step. Once the ambivalence is resolved and there is a clear desire for a relationship, it often comes very quickly. On the other hand, if we haven't done the inner work and are instead trying to find a relationship by working the numbers—lots of dates, matching services, clubbing— we may find such attempts a futile, exhausting process. Relationships often come to us when we least expect them and when on a deeper level, whether we know it or not, we have arrived at the perfect time.

In finding that part of yourself that doesn't want a romantic relationship, journaling can be useful. Start with answering, "I don't want a romantic relationship because..." Then move onto, "It would feel safe to be in a romantic relationship if..." You may be surprised by what truths come to the surface.

## Mixing yin and yang styles for manifestation

Because our society is so biased toward the masculine method of manifestation, men and women both learn how to set a goal and work externally toward it (again, the yang approach). Women have a great advantage when it comes to manifesting with the yin method, because we are often more deeply connected to the yin energy by virtue of being in a female body. Our wombs are designed to hold space for the growth of new life, so the natural energy of our bodies can help us to connect to holding space for our desired outcomes, rather than working to get them.

The long-standing work ethic of "work hard" is an old energy. The new and more effective alignment today is "work passionately". Working passionately combines the masculine (work) and feminine (passion) to create a tremendously powerful opportunity to create desired outcome.

Once a desire for something—be it a job, a relationship, a physical object, or an experience—has been identified, it is useful to consider how both the masculine and feminine forms of manifestation can be used. To access the feminine yin powers you might create a collage or picture of your desire, visualize it as already true, and immerse yourself into that joyful emotion of attainment. You might put out a request to the universe. Then, to access the masculine yang principle, you can begin to take physical action. This combination of energies can yield far greater results than either one alone.

## Recognizing your personal blend of feminine/masculine energies

I still bounce between the masculine and feminine forms of manifestation. No matter how many times I demonstrate the power of my desires, large and small, being immediately answered, I still somehow think that hard work will get results faster or better than desire. Yet, again and again, when I connect with desire, the outcome flows into my life with the utmost ease. When I focus my energy on myself and my own issues, I find my business runs better than when I "work" the traditional path of the entrepreneur.

When I remember to embrace the feminine form of manifestation, results often arrive so quickly that I don't have time to implement my multipoint action list. I've occasionally caught myself feeling stressed because I had so many clients that I didn't have time for the business-development activities that are designed to lead to more clients—now that's a problem I don't mind having!

My business slowing down often coincides with a time of personal growth and processing, and I use that time to turn inward and reflect upon my current state of being. I invariably find that as much as I love my career, at the times that the appointment book has lots of empty spaces, the quieter pace honors what truly serves me. I'm exactly where I need to be, which is quite often resting and unwinding all that active energy I can generate. The lull allows me to sit in the hot tub, curl up with a book, enjoy a movie with a friend, and refill my personal energy reserves. Then I can reconnect to my desire for more clients and submit a shamanic request, compose a list of actions to take, and the phone often begins ringing before I even take the first step!

However you approach it, making peace and honoring the masculine and feminine energies within yourself in equal measure places you in a powerful position to get what you want in life, both within yourself and from the external world.

# Chapter 16—Meeting the Masculine Divine

One of the great gifts of my shamanic practice is the chance to connect with energy in its purest form. This was especially precious when it came to connecting with masculine energy. Connecting with the masculine in shamanic reality allowed me to experience the pure, raw, archetypal energy, undiluted by human ego, pride, or insecurity. For women who have had a number of negative experiences with men, this can be an invaluable way to feel what the pure form of this energy is like. After all, if we don't have an energetic reference point, it can be confusing to try to find the manifestation in the physical world.

Experiencing the archetypal masculine energy allowed me to better discern and embrace that energy as expressed by the men in my life. Shamanic reality is also a very safe place to experience receiving from the masculine. A lot of my work with the masculine divine has taken place on the Big Island of Hawaii. It is a particularly powerful place and a great place to focus on the spiritual part of myself. In addition to receiving from and honoring the masculine, I also learned a lot about shamanic healing for the masculine.

### A message from Pele

My friend Mara and I traveled to Hawaii in June 2007. On the plane ride over, I journeyed for information about our trip. Pele, the volcano goddess of the Islands, told me that we were to work with and experience the sacred masculine energy during our time in Hawaii. She said Mara and I had done good work in the preceding years and created an anchor for the divine feminine well within ourselves. Our next step was to learn to meet the masculine energy while carrying the vibration of the divine feminine. I was told that in Hawaii, we would have the chance to meet the purest expression of the divine masculine energy. This experience would become the road map to help us find and bring forth that same energy in men.

As the trip unfolded, we had the chance to experience the wounded masculine and begin learning to work with healing that energy. In the City of Refuge, we encountered the pain and feeling of loss of manhood from those who felt they had failed to protect their sacred land, the divine mother. Near the town of Hawi, by the road, we found a solemn energy and realized that change comes slowly to the wounded masculine. And above Waipi'o we experienced what Pele described as the divine masculine.

## Making love to the divine masculine

I had always held myself back from bringing my sexual experience into shamanic reality. It felt inappropriate to include that part of myself, as though the guides working for my highest and best wouldn't be a part of that. I also had a fear of opening myself up to energies and beings who weren't working for my highest and best.

When I arrived at the top of Waipi'o Valley, my shamanic abilities were not at full strength. I had overdone the day before and my guides were strongly recommending a day of rest, recovery, soaking up joyful energy, with no more shamanic work to heal the land. Mara set up a bridge of light to guide and carry the souls who were ready to leave. As we lay on the grass, enjoying the energy, it soon became clear to me that Mara was enjoying the energy a lot more than I was. It was feeling good to me, but it was clearly feeling great to her in a very personal way.

She had connected to the land and as she did, she became aware of the sexual energy being offered by the guardian of the place. As she opened to that experience, she learned from him that he was delighted and that it had been a very long time since he had connected with a human being in that way.

Lying on the green grass of that sunny hill, it felt like the perfect time for this new experience. I ask Mara how she did this and she talked to me about inviting the energy from the land to stream up and enter her root chakra then move up through each chakra. I followed her instructions, sending out the invitation.

While Mara seemed to be having a very intense experience, I felt the Guardian of Waipi'o being very gentle with me. There was healing to be done around my sexuality. With many partners, I have asked for intensity, allowing myself to be swept away in the sexual experience, jumping over the painful sexual landscape and ahead to the pleasure. But the Guardian of Waipi'o combined healing with pleasure in equal measures, applying a soft, deep, arousing energy. I've often run my own energy circuit and enjoyed the power and pleasure of my own body. This experience of having pure, divine masculine energy come in from the outside was new and wondrous.

The energy we were running looked delicious to those passing by. Most notably, a tourist bus stopped and we received smiles, waves and cheers.

A few days later, I took a shamanic journey back to run energy again with the Guardian of Waipi'o Valley. In the journey, I got to lay back, between him and the land. As he made love to me, I was between the land itself, the divine mother, and the divine masculine, the God, the horned one. At the same time, I was the land, sinking into her, feeling myself a part of her, wrapped in vines, melting into the grass. I could feel myself part of the circuit that restored vitality to the land.

Since that time, the Guardian of Waipi'o Valley has become a regular spirit guide and helper of mine. He will hold me in shamanic reality when I am tired and needing nurturing or protection. He will run sexual energy with me when I want to be ravished. It is an expression of pure love, without any agenda. The great thing is that there's enough of him to go around, so I often invite students and clients to connect with him. Even without a shamanic journey, his energy can be invited in during meditation, self-pleasuring, or just a nice day at the beach.

## A divine father figure

Following our March 2008 retreat on the Big Island, I received another gift of connection to the masculine divine. Mara and I traveled up the volcano Mauna Kea. The air gets thin as you go up and by the time we arrived, I didn't need drumming to go into an altered shamanic state. I connected with the consciousness of the mountain. This masculine energy seemed infinitely amused and charmed with me. I had the sense of how tremendously smaller I was than this being. I knew that there was nothing I could offer him that he would want or need from me. He invited me to be as his daughter, to call upon him when I needed help, and placed me under his protection.

The pure, powerful archetypal father energy was an amazing gift. The side of his volcano is still a place I travel to in shamanic reality when I'm feeling small, weary or unprotected. In this shamanic path I walk, I often feel out on my own, guiding others. I seldom find human teachers I can follow for long. So, having an older, wiser, powerful father figure in shamanic reality fulfilled a part of myself that I didn't even realize had this yearning. The Guardian of Mauna Kea has become a cornerstone of feeling protected, safe, and loved as I travel my path.

## Meeting the masculine warriors

The last day of the March 2008 trip, Mara and I came to the Pu'ukohola Heiau, a Hawaiian temple and place of worship. It was built by Kamehameha to insure his success in conquering and uniting the Hawaiian Islands. Built near an older heiau, rocks were carried thirty miles for this Hawaiian temple.

Mara had been told, in a journey on the plane ride on the way over, that we might come to a cross, resembling bones, that seemed to say "Do not enter". The guides told her that she and I were invited to go further.

Before the heiau, just as described in Mara's journey, there was a cross of poles with large white round clothes on the end, rather like the cross bones with sculls. It was placed across the entrance to the heiau, in addition to the more conventional gate with the "Do not enter" sign. Only certain native people, with prior arrangement could go into the heiau. We talked it over and agreed that it was polite and respectful to keep our physical bodies outside. However, we sent our awareness to accept the invitation of the guides to the inside.

When I had been in Hawaii nine months before, the guides had me create a golden bridge from inland on the Island to the beach just below the heiau to allow souls to cross over, guardians to transition, and old energy to be released. It challenged me and when I arrived near the heiau, a great number of souls added themselves to the procession, greatly increasing the weight of the energy I carried. I anchored the bridge into the ocean and released it.

Human sacrifice had been practiced at this heiau, as in many other places on the Islands, so the energy lingered there. I had done work during the previous trip with the golden bridge to help heal it. This trip, as I sat outside the barrier, I did additional work. The energy was fascinating, for there was much that was good and right and powerful about the place. Men had worked together to create it. They had held sacred rituals there and formed a strong spiritual connection to being a man in community.

As Mara put it, "There was a time when men came together regularly in council, seeking each other's wisdom and support in all matters. They witnessed each other and offered assistance, solutions or silence as deemed appropriate. Their roles as men were reworked and reinforced to reflect changes in the community, family, and themselves. Their talents were acknowledged and their needs addressed. From these councils they walked back into their lives feeling enriched and whole, part of a strong brotherhood they could rely upon and to which they could contribute."

At the same time, there was wounding, trauma, and pain that came from the practice of human sacrifice.

There were many souls of men who had lived before that chose to linger at the heiau. They protected it and when I was there, they invited me in and spoke to me. I offered to help clear the energy from the human sacrifice and all that was out of alignment. They agreed and I helped the souls of the victims to cross over and removed the psychic imprint of their pain.

## Women healing men?

The warriors, for this heiau was originally a temple to the war god and a place to make ready for war, spoke to me. They said that I was being called into service to assist the wounded masculine with healing and therefore they would aid me and teach me.

"But how is it that I, a woman, am called? Isn't it better for a man to do this work?" I asked.

They responded that I was being called as one following the way of the shaman, one who walks between worlds, rather than on the basis of my gender. They said that the power and abilities that allow for a soul healing are being cultivated and explored by more women than men. Hence, the people with the ability and the willingness to answer the call are being tapped for this work, regardless of gender.

In writing this, I feel the pride and pleasure of these souls, knowing that their words and knowledge will be shared.

## Men's sacred space

These ancient Hawaiian warriors told me that this heiau was important because it was a place for men to come together and connect spiritually with being a man, along with their brothers, fathers, and sons. It was a place to honor their gods and ask for favor. It was also a place to prepare for war, to leave the distractions of everyday life behind, and become the incarnate expression of the warrior in a deep clear way. If one fell in battle, having the spiritual connection to the heiau gave the soul a place to return to. And when one returned from battle, they said the heiau was a place that they could be cleansed of the experience, to release it, to process as needed, before they went back to the more tender roles of father, brother, husband, son in everyday life.

## Ancient wisdom for modern men

As I sat in the hot sun, amid the lava rocks, the warriors spoke to me of what they saw of so many modern men. They said that to be a man is to be a solitary being in many ways. The "I" is very important and a man must know how to stand alone. They said that modern men have the same deep pull in their hearts to express the divine masculine, to express strength, protection, procreation, the ability to stand alone, to provide for loved ones. However, they said that these men are also disconnected from Spirit.

The warriors showed me an energy, held in the earth, that provided sustenance, community, fellowship beneath the feet of each man walking the solitary path. It allowed them to stand on their own, while also being deeply connected to their brothers and to the divine. It gave them guidance, a compass in the world, and a sense of connection. This was their anchor and source of strength, allowing balanced expression of the masculine traits.

These long dead Hawaiian warriors told me this energy is still held in the collective consciousness of humanity, just below our feet. They charged me to connect men to it. It will help the modern man feel sure of himself, confident, and allow him to align himself to the highest expression of the divine masculine. Instead of feeling so vulnerable in the expectations of what it is to be a man, it will allow him to relax into this space, supported by the divine. They showed me that men today are often trying to fulfill a traditional role, minus all the resources that their great grandfathers had to anchor and support them.

## Men's club—members only!?!

I had read that women were never allowed within this sacred place before I walked up to the base of the heiau. I had bristled a little at that. So, I asked the warriors about it. They smiled rather wryly and shook their heads. They told me that I misunderstood. It isn't that they didn't think women were spiritual or powerful. They said women are *so* distracting. They told me how if a woman was present, they couldn't focus on their rituals and spiritual practices, some part of them would be performing to impress her or desiring her or wondering what she thought. They implied that women are so wonderfully compelling that it was impossible to focus on anything else when they are present. Hence, they needed a space without women to prepare for war.

The warriors shared energy with me to help me to initiate, awaken, and connect men to the masculine divine within themselves and a sense of community. I suggested, when this was complete, that they would be stronger and more powerful if they completed the death process and allowed their souls to travel on and reintegrate with their higher selves. They could then return to this place, to act as guardians, with more power and wisdom at their disposal. After a discussion, they agreed to go in waves, first one group, then when they returned, the next group and so on. That way the sacred space was never left unguarded or abandoned.

## A cave experience in Hawaii

On the Big Island of Hawaii, just off the Saddle Road, are caves formed by a lava tube. Mara and I led our group of women into the caves as part of our *2008 Hawaiian Shamanic Experience.*

At the bottom of the stairs, following the lava tube to the right is a cave area that holds the energy of the divine feminine. We spent time in that cave connecting to Pele, the divine feminine energy of the land, and that energy within ourselves. We emerged as Daughters of Pele, reborn after spending time underground in the cave that symbolized her womb. Through this passageway, new earth was born from molten rock that the volcano has carried up from deep under the planet surface.

## Healing for the guardian

On the other side of the cave, the energy is masculine. There was a guardian of that cave who felt wounded and unhappy. After the time on the feminine side of the caves, we went to the masculine side. Mara and I received the message that the masculine, through contact with the healed, divine feminine, heals itself spontaneously. It's not that the feminine does anything, it's just a natural effect.

Inside the cave, I tuned into the guardian. I sat there, allowed him to be as he was, and held the thought and feeling, "I honor you." As I sat there, he slowly warmed to me. Instead of the message of "leave me alone", I could feel him beginning to move around me. If he had been in human form, he would have bustled around, made me a cup of tea, and made sure that I had a soft cushion to sit on. I felt his energy change to wanting me to be comfortable in his cave.

It felt like an old, solitary bachelor, who suddenly is left to care for a much beloved niece, but who has no idea what to do with a woman and is therefore making it up as he goes along. As the guardian extended his energy to make me comfortable, I set my intent to receive. It was a different approach, for usually I deal with spirits who are in pain by offering my services and trying to get them to accept my help. Instead, I just let him feel how delighted and honored I was by the energy he was offering.

I got the sense of him offering to hold me, and I moved slowly into that, feeling my own apprehension about letting a spirit being who wasn't one of my guides so close. It was like a man putting his arm around a woman for the first time in a long time. He's not quite sure how it goes or how it will be received. I relaxed slowly into the energy as I realized I was safe. Each time he offered energy and I accepted it and was pleased, the guardian of the cave and I came a little closer.

I moved slowly, carefully, and mindfully through my ability to let myself receive and feel safe, even with a being who wasn't perfectly healed. It gave this being a chance to have a different relationship with a human than simply those who entered his cave uninvited, snapped pictures, and sometimes left trash. In allowing him to give to me, to hold me, to keep me safe, and in my honoring of that gift, I felt him heal. By the time I left the cave, I was filled with wonderful energy and fantastic feeling. I could feel how he was more balanced, alive, and in joy.

Others of our group had similar experiences. Mara felt called to set an intent to honor the masculine in her life. One of the participants channeled a call from the guides to hold the masculine with tenderness and remember that they were once the babies and children that women held in their arms.

For me, I received the wonderful energy of being valued, fussed over, and held as dear by a large spirit. I saw that by opening myself, trusting and accepting a gift, I could offer healing. It wasn't my power that helped with the healing, it was my openness and my receptivity.

## Many flavors of the masculine

In Hawaii, I formed relationships with many different flavors of the masculine. I connected to a lover, a father, a doting uncle and a whole collection of warriors. These beings enrich my shamanic experience. They also deepen my ability to connect with the masculine divine as embodied by the men in my life—my own father, my lovers, and my male friends.

# Chapter 17—The Healing Process

Much of the healing process is about the relationship to discomfort. We choose to heal and grow, in part, because it is more uncomfortable to stay in the place we are than it is to release the ideas, emotions, and old ways of being. However, if the healing process we pick is too intense, it can be too overwhelming and staying where we are becomes more comfortable than going through the change. Sometimes going fast and hard through change is optimal. At other times, activating healing very gently is ideal, so that there isn't a great deal of discomfort—this allows us to realize that change and healing aren't so uncomfortable, so why not go down that path? Whatever path you pick, do it with love and tenderness for the part of you that is frightened of the change and of dealing with old pain.

I find that when I'm doing energy work with someone, the softer and gentler I make the energy, the more the wounded parts of their energy field will open and take in the energy. The approach of using lots of powerful energy to blast and force damage away tends to make people feel awful, sometimes creating wounds in getting to the damage that is being removed.

When embarking on a healing journey around sexuality, remember to be gentle. Rather than forcing yourself to "just get over it," think of opening your sexuality as coaxing a scared child out from under the bed. Think about how you can make it safe and comfortable to let this beautiful, authentic part of yourself out into the world.

One of the things that happens when there has been sexual trauma or when we don't actively move the energy through our body is that our energy becomes stagnate in the sexual centers. It is hard to feel sexually aroused, juicy, or yummy when there are big energy blocks.

Sometimes this happens for self-protection. If a pain or trauma is too big to be processed, it is stored in the body. If you cut off the flow of energy through the lower chakras, you won't feel the pain or damage or make yourself able to ignore it. However, this cuts you off from connecting with earth energy that nurtures and sustains. It's hard to be fully in your body and therefore fully present in the moment if you aren't anchored in the lower chakras. We tend to tuck away all kinds of pain and hurt into our lower chakras, especially the sacral and solar plexus. Truths that we swallow, pain that we stuff, emotions that we reject, all reside in this part of the body. As long as we are avoiding them, it's hard to fully experience wonderful, open, sexual energy.

## Healing for the Physical, Energetic and Soul levels

Within the human experience, there are three layers or aspects of self. There is the physical body with the heart and lungs and bones and nerves that make up this aspect of our being. This is the part that is tangible and can be touched and measured.

There is the layer of the energy body. The energy body permeates and surrounds the physical body. It holds our emotional energy, ranging from the current emotions to the pain we tucked away in our left hip when we were five. It contains our ch'i (usually pronounced *cheh*), our life force energy.

Finally there is our soul or essence. This is the part of the self that transcends the physical experience. It goes from lifetime to lifetime. When we die, this part re-integrates with our higher self until we next choose to send our awareness and part of our being back into a physical body.

In healing or opening sexuality, we can work with all these levels of the self. They are interconnected. For example, let's look at a person with severe back pain. That issue appears on each of these three levels.

The soul or essence may carry past life trauma that makes the back vulnerable or perhaps there has been soul loss that leaves an open space, causing the back to be open to an energetic intrusion. If shamanic work is done to heal these issues and the person integrates the change, then the energy body releases the trauma and, over time, the physical aligns itself to the energy body and the issue improves or disappears.

The same back issue can be addressed at the energy body level. If the person begins doing Qi Gong (usually pronounced *cheh kongh*), Reiki, acupuncture, or visualization on the back and begins moving the energy, over time, the physical must align with the energy body. Just as an imbalance in the energy body causes the physical body to misalign over time, manifesting illness, pain and disease, the healthy, flowing energy body causes the physical to become healthier. Likewise, the healthy energy body informs the soul or essence level, causing whatever trauma or pain is held on that level to release.

When we process emotions, the pain that has been held in the emotional body is released and that allows the energy to begin to flow again, creating a healing ripple that resonates through the physical and soul levels. In fact, when I experience a major emotional healing, I often get a physical detox because my body is releasing the physical element in the form of toxins that were held due to my unresolved emotional baggage.

And, of course, when the physical body becomes healthier, the energetic body aligns to that health, which, in turn, causes the essence or soul to change to reflect the new condition. So, if someone does good core exercise or physical therapy, aligning and strengthening the physical body, this healing and strengthening is reflected through the other layers.

All these levels—the soul, the energy body, and the physical body—strive to be in alignment with each other. When one of them changes, the entire energy systems works to synchronize these three levels in whatever way is easiest. So, persistent emotional imbalance often results in physical issues and getting emotionally healthier can create healing in the physical body.

Because a healing on one level is being integrated on all three levels, persistence is often required. When I teach my Reiki students about channeling this universal healing energy, I tell them that a one-time injury responds much faster to Reiki energy than a chronic problem. If you hurt your arm then apply energy healing, the energy body and the soul or essence are still aligned with a healthy arm and the body uses the energy to move the physical quickly back to that alignment. However, if someone has knee problems for a decade, they may get immediate relief from something that puts the energy body into a healthy alignment, such as acupuncture or Reiki, but if it's not done regularly, the body may return to the original state of illness.

With the kissing quest, I changed my energetic self. By getting to where I felt safe and comfortable with sexual energy, I could start to appreciate how delicious it is. So, instead of running an emotional energy of fear and protection in the face of sexual energy, I began to experience joy and delight. As this energy of excitement and delight flowed, it allowed old energy of fear to be canceled and cleared. As my emotional body relaxed and delighted in sexual energy, my physical body became more open to sex, my energetic body began releasing trauma, and my soul began letting go of patterns that didn't match an open, joyful sexuality.

## Working on the appropriate level

While healing on all levels can happen with any one level—physical, energy body, or soul—it is often most efficient to work on more than one level at the same time. Also, with some problems, the damage is deep or intense enough that it is very difficult to effect healing without working directly with the appropriate level. For some physical ailments, it is most powerful, effective and necessary to see your Western medical doctor. If I have pneumonia, I take antibiotics first, then talk to my guides about what is out of alignment in my life that caused me to be vulnerable. Sometimes things are so far out of alignment on the physical that the change must occur there. The inertia or resistance is just too high for changing the energy to make a complete difference on the physical level.

Likewise, if the emotional or sexual trauma has been too great and caused a great deal of soul loss, getting back those pieces and clearing the pattern on that level is something that's difficult to accomplish without something like direct shamanic work. It can be done—great healing of the physical and emotional and energy bodies can lead to spontaneous soul return. However, just like trying to get rid of pneumonia through meditation is uphill work, direct shamanic healing can be the fastest, most powerful path to deep healing.

## When everything aligns

I worked with a woman who had severe back pain for eight years. She had tried Reiki, surgery, chiropractic, acupuncture, magnets, crystals, and a number of other modalities that I'd never heard of. I did a shamanic journey and removed energy that had become stuck in her lower back. I went into her past lives and cleared all the experiences she'd had of damage to that area in other lifetimes. I anchored a destiny path of healing for this area. I got specific suggestions from her guides about how to manage her emotions—anger, despair, bitterness—about the pain so that it wouldn't impact the healing process. I heard from her later that right after the healing session, for the first time in eight years, the chronic pain was gone.

Timing is everything: I had the good fortune to work with her at the point that she was deeply ready to release this pain. Her guides brought her to me because this was the most effective tool at that moment to effect her healing. For another person with back pain, the right physical therapist might hold the optimal transformational opportunity.

The exercises and techniques I suggest for healing and awakening sexuality are ways to work with various levels of the being. Any one will promote growth and healing. A combination creates an even more powerful effect. Pick the ones that feel the best to you.

## CHAPTER 18—HOW TO DEAL WITH STRONG EMOTION

So much of healing around sexuality, in relationships and in our lives in general depends on how we walk though emotions. When emotions are not processed, they create toxicity in our energy fields, disconnect us from our power and deplete our life force energy.

Many people find that it is impossible to really open to and experience sex with large amounts of unresolved emotion. When we have sex, the pleasure makes us come home to ourselves, be in our bodies, connect to our energy field. There are ways around this, of course, such as drinking or sex without intimacy. But, while those can be fun, it's worthwhile to have the full expression.

### Some techniques

I've worked with a lot of techniques for dealing with uncomfortable emotions. It wasn't a natural skill of mine, but I quickly found it vital to having the kind of life I want. Feel free to pick and choose whatever works for you.

*Anger: Wisdom for Cooling the Flames* by Thich Nhat Hanh contains a great way of dealing with strong, difficult emotions. He talks about taking care of the anger (or other feeling) as though it was a baby. By being present with the emotion, holding it, honoring it, being concerned with it, the feeling is resolved and released. His instruction is clear and loving. He provides wonderful instructions for meeting yourself.

I'm also a huge fan of Pema Chodron's tonglen instruction. She has a number of books and CDs. The tonglen practice is particularly wonderful for people who struggle with strong emotions. As we become aware of the difficult energies created by dwelling in pain, metaphysical seekers can get panicky when they find themselves stuck in anger or sadness. If we understand we manifest with our emotions, it can be scary to have these feelings that might undermine our goals for abundance and joy in the world.

In the tonglen practice, instead of trying to get rid of uncomfortable feelings or push them away, you go directly into them. So, for example, if I'm angry at my boyfriend, instead of avoiding the feelings by telling stories about how he's bad, or having a drink to avoid the feelings, or trying to push them away, I breathe into the anger. Perhaps sadness or fear come up and I breathe into those as well. With tonglen, on the in breath you breathe into the painful feeling and allow yourself to feel it fully. On the out breath, you send relief to yourself and everyone else who is experiencing the same emotion. It's a beautiful practice that reminds us that we are not alone in our most painful moments. It allows us to shift our energy between the pain and the higher intent, which helps the energy of the emotion to flow and change and release. It is a great relief for me to find a way to be with my anger, judgment, and woundedness in a way that is spiritual and connected to the universe. I seek relief for everyone by embracing my own pain.

## When strong emotions are combined with trauma

Sometimes emotions and pain are simply too big and it's important to get some help to facilitate their release. This is especially good if there has been trauma. Conventional therapy can be very useful for this. In addition, there are some great new therapeutic techniques to help people release trauma very efficiently. Somatic Experiencing is a technique that helps the body to release trauma. It is extremely powerful and can have a great effect in just a few sessions. EMDR, which stands for Eye Movement Desensitization and Reprocessing is an extremely effective treatment for post-traumatic stress disorder and other release of trauma. Somatic experience and EMDR are great in that they work very quickly, require minimal story, and simply eliminate trauma from the body and psyche.

## Tenderness towards the self

Just being present with the feeling and thinking about it in terms of where you feel it in your body, what it might look like, how it might change over time can be a good way to help release strong emotions. All too often, when we're upset, we tend to make up stories, remember past events, and say things to ourselves that cause more pain. Even if it's true that your current relationship mirrors something from your childhood, when you're hurting, it can be better just to sit with the purple and black lump than tell yourself how you're always abandoned.

Inner child work is extremely powerful for dealing with strong emotions. Imagine that you're the parent you wish you'd had. Get an image of you holding yourself in the way that you'd like to be held. Allow that part of you to have whatever feelings there are and say the kind of loving, tender things you'd say to a child in pain. Like, "Honey, it's okay. I love you. I'm right here. I'm going to take care of you. I know it hurts now, but this will pass. I'm not going to leave you. You're safe." You may be amazed at how some tenderness towards yourself will help relieve these feelings. If you're struggling to find a grown up part of yourself, you can call in guides or power animals or the divine to hold you in your pain.

I find it helpful to make a list of people that I trust with my vulnerable self at a time when I'm feeling good. When I'm hurting, it's easy to feel utterly alone. Then I can open up my list on my computer of people I love and trust and think about who I might want to call or write when my heart hurts. It helps when my closest friends aren't available for some reason. I find friends that can just hold space and hear my pain without taking sides and assigning blame are the most helpful when I hurt.

## Additional tools

Ester and Jerry Hicks talk, in their books and recordings, about the Emotional Scale. The idea is that no one can reliably go straight from misery to joy. You need to raise your emotional vibration a little at a time. So if you hurt, instead of trying to be happy the next moment, you might think about ease and relief. Anger is an emotional step up from depression, for example. It may be more uncomfortable, but it's more life-affirming.

I get a lot out of Byron Katie's work. Her method is one of asking yourself four questions that are very powerful for questioning the painful stories we tell ourselves. It helps me to not take things personally. For example, I might feel, "My boyfriend doesn't love me". I would ask myself it that's true and whether I can absolutely know it's true. I then acknowledge that I don't know if it's true. I examine who I would be without that thought. I then turn it around and see if other things are equally or more true. "My boyfriend does love me." "I love me." "I don't love me." It's a method that breaks down painful stories and belief systems and helps me to make peace with reality.

Sometimes dealing with a strong emotion can be as simple as breathing into it and following the breath. Richard Bock has a great CD called Quantum Light Breath that is a wonderful guided journey of breathing and releasing. Without a sound track, or someone to hold space for me and help me stay on task, I find it very easy to lose track of my intent for breathing into the feeling. When I lose focus I can wander off into stories and mental distraction, so I like having the CD.

## Being in your body

Coming back to your body is very helpful. One of the things that happens when we get used to running a certain emotional program is that we fall into the groove of telling ourselves a painful story, reacting in a certain way, and getting stuck. This might happen to someone who gets cut off on the freeway or thwarted in some way who always responds with the thought, "You can't trust anyone, people will always hurt you." This thought and reaction gets worn into a groove, so finding ways to disrupt those kind of ideas and victim type thoughts can create a powerful healing and life change.

Physical movement and exercise are great for transmuting strong emotions. When you move the body, you move your energy and it makes it hard for painful emotions to get stuck. It's difficult to be deeply depressed with regular exercise. Meditation or shamanic journey can also be great ways to move your energy and state of being, allowing for the peaceful release of challenging emotions.

One of my students shared her technique when she gets angry of visualizing a monster in a room that throws a fit and destroys everything around it. It creates a safe space to allow the feeling to be expressed, without taking it out on those around her.

Whatever technique you find works for you, I strongly recommend doing it with a conscious intent to transmute and release the energy back to life force energy. By spending some of your intent on "cleaning up" the energy you release, you won't find yourself bogged down in it later. This could be burning sage, playing music, lighting a candle, taking a salt bath, or using some other technique that makes you think of releasing and clearing old, unhelpful energy. Also, it's very important to make sure that you're not sending your painful energy to anyone else. My book, *Practical Shamanism: A Guide for Walking in Both Worlds* deals with this in greater detail.

## Taking action

For me, the challenge with any of these techniques for dealing with my strong emotions is getting myself to take action. To release and clear these emotions, I need to become present with them and acknowledge them, which is the opposite of my instinct to run away from pain. It takes a lot of discipline to be present with myself when I hurt, physically or emotionally. So, whatever baby steps you're able to take in this regard, remember to pat yourself on the back and honor your courage. And, don't hesitate to take a class or find another person to help facilitate this process. The rewards are huge; more energy, greater joy, ease in setting and holding boundaries, increased self-esteem and more grace in the world.

# Chapter 19—Exercises: Connecting with Spirit Guides and Archetypes

As a shamanic practitioner, whenever I embark on a new endeavor, I often ask the question, "Who is here to help me?" Many times I will journey to ask for a new guide to support me in something new that I'm undertaking, whether it's a romantic relationship, learning belly dance, or an effort to increase my business.

## Inviting spirit guides

In embarking on a deeper opening of your sexuality, it is helpful to invite in a divine presence to assist and support you. Having a spirit guide can help connect you to the grace and beauty of the experience. A guide can help increase your ability to connect with wonderful people to help you grow and to find delight along the way. This connection can help open a path of ease and grace. A guide can help you feel clarity, keep a higher perspective, and deepen your intuition. Basically, your guide is constantly working with the energy, behind the scenes, to help you with your goals.

As a shamanic practitioner, naturally I'm a huge advocate of learning the basic skill set of shamanic journey, allowing you to move into an altered state to meet your guide personally. My book, *Practical Shamanism: A Guide for Walking in Both Worlds* provides detailed instruction on how to journey. Using a specific drumbeat, the practitioner moves into an altered state to consult with spirit guides and themselves. One of the most powerful aspects of shamanic journey is that while in that light trance state, you can access both your conscious and unconscious self, simultaneously. It is a conscious form of self-hypnosis, allowing you to work directly with the unconscious mind to release trauma, activate growth and promote healing.

If you embark on a shamanic journey, you would travel to your sacred garden or to upper world with the intention "I want to meet the guide that will assist me in deepening my connection to my sexuality." Other intents could include asking for a guide to assist with healing, a guide to help you connect to the sacredness of this aspect of your being, or a guide to assist you in connecting to a partner that will help you discover a richer aspect of yourself.

## Meeting your goddess guide

There are many other ways to connect with your spirit guide to support you in this aspect of your life. I recommend connecting specifically with a goddess archetype. It makes it easier to connect with the divine nature of your sexuality and your deep power as a woman. In inviting in this guide, it is helpful to start with a statement of intent. Some examples:

"I want to connect with the goddess who is an ally for my highest and best good as I explore, awaken and deepen my sexual self."

"I invite the goddess to work with me who will best support me in coming into my power, honoring my sexuality and/or healing from trauma."

Whatever the statement, the asking creates an opening and an invitation for a spirit guide to come into relationship with you. Because free choice is honored and sacred, spirit guides, angels, and the divine are limited in the action they can take on our behalf in the absence of specific invitation and permission. In other words, to get more help, you have to ask.

Once you are clear and have put together your request, you have several options for connecting with a goddess guide. You can read about different goddesses and find one that resonates for you. When you select the goddess that feels like the best fit, you can specifically ask that she come into relationship with you. The great thing about the spiritual world is that we get the flavor of the archetype that is perfect for us, so while my Isis may have different energies than your Isis, she is available to both of us, in the perfect way for our spiritual path.

When you choose to come into relationship with a goddess by selecting the one to invite, you will deepen the connection by honoring that goddess in your life in some way. For example, if you pick an earth goddess, you can acknowledge her with your recycling or water conservation efforts. You can also strengthen the connection by putting up an image of her or burning a candle on her behalf. For instance, when I've needed extra protection in my home, I'll burn a candle to the Virgin de Guadalupe.

Likewise, pay attention to the strengths and attributes of the goddess you select. For example, if you want to cultivate compassion for yourself and others, Kuan Yin (often pronounced or written *Guanyin*) is a great ally. If, on the other hand, you are connecting to the woman warrior aspect, Kuan Yin is perhaps not the best match. Kali, Hindu goddess of creation and destruction, or Morrigan (usually pronounced *mohree'gan*), Celtic goddess of war, might be a better fit.

Another way is to look for the goddess who wants to come to you. You can do this by getting a book of goddesses or a deck of goddess cards. State your intent for connecting to the appropriate goddess guide then draw a card or open the book at random. That is the goddess that is coming to you.

You can also use other approaches like asking to see a name or indicator of your goddess three times or inviting her to meet you and make herself known to you in the dreamtime.

A basic meditation is another way to connect. Begin with the "Roots into the Ground" exercise described later in this chapter. Then imagine walking down a path to a pool of water. In your mind's eye, stand at the water's edge and make your request for your goddess guide. See ripples appear in the center of the pool and watch her rise up to meet you. As she rises, the pool changes, perhaps it becomes crystal or fire, whatever element your goddess is most at home with. Open yourself to feel her energy and receive a message. The message may be delivered with words or simply become a knowing in your heart. When you feel complete, imagine walking back down the path that you came along. See yourself again with roots in the earth. Take a few deep breaths and return your awareness to the normal world.

It's helpful to keep a journal regarding your goddess guide and your experiences. I see people have some amazing spiritual experiences yet when they are feeling stressed or sad or overwhelmed, it's hard to call to mind the magical experiences. Having a record can be a good reality check if you ever feel disconnected from Spirit. It also allows you to see the road that you have traveled.

Once you have connected with your goddess guide, you can begin building a relationship. The more you talk to her, ask for her help, and reach out, the more she can assist you and the stronger the relationship becomes. As I mentioned, you might put her image about you, write down her name, or develop a simple daily ritual to honor her, like lighting incense or a candle or ringing a bell. Perhaps you will select a piece of jewelry that reminds you of this goddess connection. Consider how you embody this goddess and connect to her within you.

One of the goddesses who is especially powerful to invite along your journey as a woman connecting to her sexuality is Isis. She is an archetype of feminine power and mystery. She has been worshiped throughout the ages and has had many priestesses in her service. Connecting with Isis is a good way to access the High Priestess energy within. When we connect with the Priestess energy and our sexuality at the same time, it allows us to connect to the deep knowing that our bodies, our energy, our sexuality is sacred.

Another powerful goddess is Brigid. She is a warrior, a healer, and a hearth goddess of Celtic origin. She supports women in coming into their power, finding their voice, and connecting to the feminine divine within with the three-fold aspects of maiden, mother, and crone.

For my sexual energy, I work with a blending of support and energy from Pele, the volcano goddess of Hawaii and Kuan Yin, the Buddhist goddess of compassion. They blend red and white energy.

## Meeting Pele

I connected with Pele in Hawaii, where her energy is awake and active. Pele provides a delicious antidote to the diluted, disempowered idea of the feminine energy. No one can make Pele into a neat, tame, domestic goddess. She took her lovers where she wished and woe to anyone who stood in her way! As a volcano goddess, Pele holds the raw, primal power of creation and destruction. In connecting with Pele, I had expected intensity. I was surprised to find how deeply nurturing her energy and presence are for me. She is a powerful protector and a maternal figure. In one of my journeys to connect with her, she placed sacred lava into my womb to gently burn away old stagnate energy and to increase the flame of my life force energy. When I'm feeling depleted, I will go to Pele to have the energy of this lava refreshed and reactivated.

## Connecting with the masculine divine

You can use the same techniques to invite and connect with a god or masculine divine archetype. Connecting with a spirit guide who embodies the Divine Masculine can be immensely healing for women who have not found that energy particularly present in their life. This guide could hold the energy of a lover, a father, a brother, or a friend.

## Inviting in a power animal

Another wonderful opportunity for support is to connect with a power animal. Power animals are spirit guides in animal form. It is believed that when a child is born, a benevolent spirit in animal form looks at the infant and sees how helpless they are. That spirit takes pity on the child and becomes their ally and protector. Often a person's power animal will be an animal that they have a strong affinity for. When someone collects bear or horse figures, it's a good bet that that animal is their power animal.

In everyday life, a power animal is a source of protection and power. It's your power animal's job to make sure that the idiot driving way too fast doesn't hit you and that if a rock falls out of the sky it lands next to you, not on you. They work on our behalf to keep the physical world safe and positive for us. A loss or lack of a power animal can result in everything from listlessness to being accident prone to chronic illnesses. A strong connection to a power animal provides a source of energy and support and enhances the flow of your own energy.

As of the writing of this book, if you sign up for my mailing list, I will identify one of your power animals. You can also ask your power animal to meet you in the dreamtime, use a deck of animal cards to investigate which animals come to you, or invite a specific animal to work with you.

Because healing and opening of sexuality works with the lower chakras, power animals are particularly well suited to aid and assist us along this journey.

## Exercises

The following exercises are intended as guidelines and recommendations for finding your own healing practice. Try the ones that speak to you. Please note that these can initiate a powerful healing process. Moderation is good if there has been trauma or if these kinds of exercises are new to you. If you find yourself getting overwhelmed by the emotion that gets stirred up, don't hesitate to seek out some additional support, either from a healing practitioner or a conventional therapist. It's important to be gentle with yourself in this kind of work. At the same time, a regular application of one or more of these exercises can be life changing.

The release of pain, trauma, and old energy can also result in a physical detox, such as flu-like symptoms and intestinal stuff, like loose stool or diarrhea. This doesn't happen often, but it can occur when the body integrates a deep healing. If you've stirred up a lot of emotion or a physical reaction, refer to the chapter on dealing with strong emotion for some tips. Focus on self-nurturing and inner child work when you're feeling vulnerable.

## Preparation

The following exercise can be done on its own or as a preparation for any of the other exercises or meditations that follow. It can be done quickly with a few breaths in the middle of the day at work. (Going into the bathroom is a good opportunity to ground and center if you get overwhelmed or stressed.)

## Roots into the ground

One of the best visualizations involves mindfully connecting to the earth. It's easy for busy, worried, distracted people to get disconnected from the physical body. It's exhausting to go through the day not connected to your body and leaves you vulnerable to everything from toe stubbing to picking up other people's energy. Furthermore, the earth itself is a tremendous source of energy. Once I went through a process of healing and opening my lower chakras, I experienced a dramatic increase in my energy. I didn't get as tired, I could go for longer, I didn't get sick as often, and when I did get tired, I recovered more quickly.

This simple visualization brings you back into your body, gives you extra energy, and opens up your lower chakras. Why do you need your lower chakras open? In addition to sexuality, they are the sources of your power, passion, and will. The power and ability to accomplish things, to stand up for yourself, to hold good boundaries, to know what you want and need, are found within your lower three chakras- the root, the sacral and the solar plexus. They are the seat of your self-esteem, of valuing yourself, and of acting on your own behalf. They also support the health of many of your internal organs—liver, kidneys, digestive, elimination, and your sexual and reproductive health.

To do this visualization in the simplest form, visualize roots growing down into the earth from the bottom of your feet and from your root chakra. See them going deep into the earth. See these roots going down to whatever level feels best- whether it's the rich, damp top soil, the hard granite rock, or the molten lava. They can even go through all three.

If you're not visual, simply pretend that the roots are there, feel what it feels like. The idea of this visualization is not to see perfect roots, but rather to put your attention on your connection to the earth and the energy exchange with the earth for anywhere from a few breaths, to a few minutes, to fifteen minutes if you're really an over-achiever. There's no way to do this wrong; it's the genuine intent, not the perfect application, which will serve you.

Once you have your sense or picture or just intent that you have these energetic roots in the ground, begin to pay attention to your breath. When you breathe out, imagine any old, stagnant, unhelpful, painful energy leaving your body through the roots. Then breathe in and imagine earth energy coming into your body through the roots. If it's helpful, you can imagine a color of your choosing. I like to see this energy as green or brown or red. Do this for whatever amount of time is appropriate.

## Adding on layers to the root visualization

There are a number of pieces that you can add onto the previous visualization of roots into the ground that will make it more powerful.

Going outside is a great help. If you get your bare feet against the ground, you strengthen your earth connection. Likewise, leaning up against a tree while doing this will further empower the experience. In general, touching a tree at any time when you are feeling depleted is a great practice for instant energy balancing.

In addition to seeing roots going down from your feet and root chakra, you can add roots from each of your chakras, one at a time. So, you'd start by sending down roots from your feet, then from your root chakra (located at your perineum, between your genitals and your rectum), then from your sacral chakra (located immediately in front of the base of your spine or tail bone, about two inches below your belly button), then from your solar plexus (located just below your sternum, at the base of your diaphragm), then down from your heart chakra (located in the center of your chest, under and surrounding your physical heart), then from your throat chakra (above your thyroid and below your larynx in your throat), then from your third eye chakra (located in the center of your forehead, above your optic nerves, just above your eyebrows), and finally from your crown chakra (found at the fontanelle, or the 'soft spot' you had at infancy, at the top of your head). From here, breathe in and out, releasing energy and drawing new energy in along with the breath. This is a good one to do if you're struggling to feel grounded even after doing the basic root visualization.

Another variation that I often use starts with the root visualization. Then I visualize branches going up into the sky from my crown chakra. I see these branches as connected to universal source energy. So, I am simultaneously drawing down universal source energy and pulling up earth energy into my body.

For a deeper energetic clearing, I may use the roots in the earth and branches into the sky. I imagine and feel myself filled with earth and sky energy then imagine opening all my pores so that the energy flows into me then out through all my pores, cleaning and clearing energy of my body. When this feels complete, I close my pores and allow the energy from earth and sky to flow until I feel energetically full.

## Meditation/Shamanic journey to connect with your inner child

The following steps can be done simply as a meditation or imaginary process or as part of a shamanic journey. The advantage of doing this work as a shamanic journey is that the power of the experience can be greatly increased by doing it with your conscious and unconscious mind activated. Even if you're not doing a shamanic journey, you can use the shamanic journey drumming softly in the background to deepen your experience.

As a meditation, begin by doing the "Roots into the Ground" exercise. Close your eyes and follow your breath for a few moments. Then imagine walking down a path to meet your inner child. Travel until you find a spot that feels safe and comfortable. If you're a visual person, you may see a lot of detail in your mind's eye. If not, don't let that distract you, just imagine that you're sitting somewhere safe and comfortable. It might be a forest glade or a place by a campfire.

Invite your inner child to meet you. Open to a sense of what age child wants to talk to you today. See an image or just get a sense of that child being present with you. Sit in silence for a while, just getting the feel of being together. Then consider asking your child part some questions. "How are you?" "What makes you happy?" "What do you like to experience in my life today?" "What don't you enjoy in my life today?" "How can I take better care of you?" "What wisdom and gifts do you have for me?" These questions are guidelines, rather than a process to be memorized.

Ask the questions and just wait for the answer to arise. Think about what might make it safe for some part of you to tell the truth. Set an intent that any truth will be honored. Recognize that you have the freedom to negotiate with your child self, just as a responsible, loving parent would. You can set boundaries and talk to your child about letting you handle the grownup stuff.

Connecting with this part of yourself is often a way to connect to your joy, passion, and delight in being alive. It is easy to structure our lives in ways that don't create time for play and fun. In fact, you may have no idea how to play. Developing that skill and the balance between doing adult, productive things and joyful, experiential things can enrich your life and health.

If the visualization doesn't work to connect with your inner child, or you want to approach it in another way, try journaling. Write your questions with your dominant hand then write your child's answers with your non-dominant hand. You may be surprised what kind of answers arise and how easily they come to you. If you've had a lot of trauma, this process may be best done with a therapist to provide extra support while you're working through this.

You can also work with your inner child by simply visualizing holding him or her. Pausing when you're feeling scared, angry, or overwhelmed to say reassuring things to yourself and to send yourself a little love can have a profound impact on how you experience events that otherwise may have negative effects on your happiness and peace of mind.

## Create a sacred vessel

When I began teaching my Spiral Goddess class, I was guided to give each woman a glass vessel to symbolize her intentions for the class. We put objects into our vessels—beads, rose petals, crystals, words on paper. The guides had me talk about these vessels as a metaphor for our lives. They showed me that at some point these glass containers might be filled with objects and that in order to add new things, we would need to take things out of our vessel. The laws of the energetic world, like the physical world, dictate that an empty space must be created by removing something before something new can be put into its place.

Create a sacred vessel by choosing a glass container that speaks to you. Then put objects, pictures, words, whatever into it to symbolize the energies that you wish to be surrounded by and experience in your life. You can burn a candle on or near this vessel to strengthen your intent. It is a way to remind yourself and let spirit know what you wish to bring into your life.

## Reconciling the masculine and feminine within

This exercise can be done as a shamanic journey or a meditation. To do this as a shamanic journey, go to your sacred garden and work with your guides to help you talk to and balance the masculine and feminine within you.

Another way to do this exercise involves starting a dialog between your masculine and feminine. Consider that your feminine is your intuitive, receptive, emotional, still, yin part of your being. The masculine is your active, doing, creating, yang part of your being. Often times we end up with an inner conflict between our masculine and feminine sides, where the masculine tries to drive the feminine into being more active and productive or we get stuck in the stillness of the feminine emotions and stop being able to take action. Depression is an excess yin or feminine energy condition; stressful overachieving is an excess yang or masculine energy condition.

Spend some time writing about what each side, the masculine and feminine, would have to say about how they work, what they want, and how they are experiencing the other half. You can start with either one, but make sure you give equal time to both. You will likely find it easier to hear the voice of one side or the other. You may find that you have greater discomfort with one side than the other, in which case, you can deepen the healing by further dialog and shadow work. If you can come to allowing both parts to be exactly as they are, and love and honor both, then much of the critical internal self-talk will dissipate.

## Take it a step further

Imagine what your perfect relationship would look like between a man and a woman. Try to expand this definition out beyond romantic love to include father/daughter, mother/son, brother/sister, friendship. Write about what this connection would look like.

Then, explore on paper how the masculine and feminine can work together in the harmonious way you just explored within yourself. For example, instead of the masculine nagging the feminine to quit being lazy and do more, the masculine might accomplish work efficiently and make plans to create time for the feminine to just be still. Instead of criticizing the masculine within for mistakes, the feminine could offer intuitive suggestions and help manage the energy surrounding the projects of the masculine.

Creating harmony within the self creates a blueprint for having harmony between men and women. For example, if I'm struggling with a critical voice that dishonors my feminine side as not being active enough, not doing enough, and therefore being bad, I will be very sensitive to any hint on my partner's part that I'm not doing enough and furthermore, very critical of them not doing enough. If I've made peace with the balance between being and doing, I will be able to deal with my partner much more clearly and not take things personally.

## Balancing the masculine and feminine energies

Balancing our masculine and feminine energies allows us to access the best of both in any effort or situation. It creates a greater abundance of energy and sense of internal peace and harmony.

One way to do this involves using the deck of cards called the "Medicine Cards" which show different animals. Shuffle the deck and ask spirit to help connect you with the animals to help you balance your masculine and feminine sides. Then draw a card with your left hand and another right your right hand. Turn them over and look at the animals then invite their medicine to come into you to balance your masculine and feminine sides. If you're right handed, the left hand is considered to be the feminine and the right hand to be the masculine. You can just hold the cards in your hand for a few moments or set them out to look at during the day. If you don't want to purchase a deck of cards, make your own with names of animals on pieces of paper or draw images.

You can also do this exercise with the elements. Traditionally water and earth are considered to be feminine. Fire and air are considered to be masculine. You can hold something that represents a masculine element in your dominant hand (right hand for most people) and something that symbolized the feminine in your non-dominant hand (the left hand for most).

- Earth- stones, dirt, plants, green or brown objects
- Air- feathers, chimes, yellow or white objects
- Water- water, mirrors, blue or black objects
- Fire- fire, red or orange objects

There are many different objects- crystals, spices, etc. that correspond to different elements. You can even write the name of the element on a piece of paper or draw a picture and hold those in the appropriate hand.

## More visualizations

Visualization is a great tool. People shrink and dissolve tumors with their minds. Biofeedback trains people to use their mind to calm their body, lower their blood pressure, and release physical pain. Using the power of your mind, you can transform your emotional, physical and energetic experiences.

My friend and fellow shamanic practitioner, Mara Clear Spring, has taught me some great visualizations.

## Eighth Chakra

One of them involves drawing back the pieces of energy that we leave behind in normal daily life. Begin with the "Roots into the Ground" visualization. Then focus on your eighth chakra, located about six to eight inches above the top of your head. See the ball of energy filled with a white or rich purple color (or the color that feels right for you). Think of all the energy you've left behind, given away, or lost recently. Don't go through the details, just focus on this for 15 seconds or so. Then imagine that energy coming back to you and into your eighth chakra. Once it has been gathered up and become a large ball, see that energy become cleared and purified by the energy of the universe that is held in your eighth chakra. All energy stamps and impressions are removed. Once the purification is complete, visualize the energy flowing into the crown of your head and flowing throughout your body, to whatever place in your body or energy field is most appropriate.

Take a few deep breaths, acknowledging the feeling of having your energy back. Express a "Thank you" to the universe for the support in reclaiming your energy. Then go on about your day. Please note, this exercise is about bringing personal energy or ch'i back home. It's not effective as a substitute for soul retrieval.

## Opening and clearing the chakras

Begin with the "Roots into the Ground" visualization. Then imagine you could look at each chakra in turn and see what's there. One at a time, send your awareness to your chakra and request whatever changes seem to be needed. Perhaps there is too little energy—then draw more in from the earth. Perhaps there are dark blockages, see them being washed away. Perhaps the chakra has stopped spinning, imagine it beginning to spin again, first counter clockwise to clear it, then clockwise to draw in and flow the energy. You can do one chakra at a time or work on all of them in one sitting.

Mara taught me an exercise that involves pulling the knots out the chakras. In this exercise, imagine that there is a string coming out of the chakra. Place your hand as though it were holding that string and begin to imagine pulling on it. Be very gentle and imagine drawing out knots in the string out of the chakra, leaving it open and clear. You may want to use both hands, one after the other as you draw on this imaginary string. While this seems like a subtle exercise, it can have a profound effect. If you haven't been doing regular energy work or chakra clearing, it can be wise to do one chakra at a time. Otherwise this can create a significant detox or emotional release.

## Healing through movement

The following work simultaneously with the energy body and the physical body:

### Qi Gong

Qi Gong is a fabulous and extremely efficient way to move through energetic blocks. It promotes health and longevity. There are many different forms, some using breathing techniques, some just using movement. Most of the exercises are very gentle and, when done regularly, make a tremendous difference in health and vitality. In addition to clearing blocks in the body, Qi Gong is great for clearing emotional energy that gets stuck. Fifteen to thirty minutes a day of Qi Gong can be absolutely life changing. There's a medical center in China that works with terminally ill patients and treats them with Qi Gong. They regularly see a full recovery in patients that conventional medical practitioners expect to die.

Qi Gong will open up all the energy channels of your body and provide many benefits as well as healing and opening of the sexual channels. It is a gentle way to clear away and release emotional pain as well as physical disease.

### Belly dance
Belly dance is a great way to get energy moving into the lower chakras. It strengthens the core muscles and is excellent for overall health. As the dancer learns to isolate different muscle groups, there is a process of coming home to the body in a powerful way. Furthermore, if you choose to perform, whether it's formally or informally, there's a chance to run sexual energy with an audience in a safe way. Much like the kissing quest gave me the chance to experience sexual energy on my terms, dancing can allow you to be admired sexually, in a safe way, surrounded by friends. Belly dance is one of the most focused ways to work on flowing energy for the clearing and opening of the lower chakras.

### Yoga and Tai Chi
Yoga and Tai Chi (usually pronounced *tye jee*) are also great for moving energy while strengthening the body.

I remember reading that it's very hard to feel intense fear while the body is physically relaxed. The emotional and physical are intertwined. The idea was that if you are feeling afraid and you relax the body, the emotion of fear will dissipate. So, as you exercise and strengthen your body, especially with a form of exercise that moves the energy in a balanced way, it simply becomes impossible to hold onto certain kinds of pain.

While some additional work may be needed for optimal openness and sexuality, a regular practice that moves the body and moves the energy will create healing transformation all on its own.

## Specifically moving sexual energy
The techniques described above create energetic and physical health and balance, with a side effect of healing and awakening of sexuality. There are also some techniques that awaken and open sexual energy directly. If you have a history of abuse, be especially aware of being kind to yourself. These techniques move a lot of sexual energy, very

quickly. This can trigger some strong emotional reactions. If you have the support system and skills to move through these reactions and this feels good, by all means, go for it. But if the experience becomes too intense, I recommend using some gentler techniques when you start out.

## Tantra work

Tantra is a wonderful way of moving sexual energy and connecting to it. Tantra is a path of spiritual sexuality. There is a great range of tantric practices, ranging from running your own energy, to intercourse with a partner. For someone who has had sexual trauma, I recommend investigating "White Tantra" first. This provides practices for accessing your own sexual energy with meditation and breathing practices, without a partner. It's a very direct way to open and access sexual healing. An all women's class or a book can be a very safe way to begin.

Red Tantra refers to tantric practices that are done with a partner. This can be way too much energy for someone who is sensitive or on a healing path. Discernment is important about the people who are participating and the people who are holding space. I've often been drawn to explore more tantra, only to recognize that some of the people participating simply didn't have an energy that felt safe for me to open sexually to. Some of the men in the tantric community have felt creepy to me, not bad, but not very healed. My instinct is to reinforce my personal shields and boundaries, not open around them. I've honored that by choosing my tantra partners very carefully.

### Pelvic rock

A simple tantric practice involves a pelvic rock combined with breath. Begin by sitting on the floor. Breathe in and rock your hips forward, arching your back slightly. Breathe out and rock your pelvis the other direction, tucking your tail bone under. Repeat this breath cycle, allowing your body to move with your pelvis as feels appropriate. This exercise will move a lot of energy very quickly.

## Tantric energy circuit

In the tantric energy circuit, you move energy around your body. This exercise connects and balances your chakras and moves energy into an even flow throughout your body. It helps bring your energy system into harmony.

Begin by sitting in a comfortable position. If it is comfortable and feels appropriate for you, sit in a way that your spine is straight, shoulders back and down. Place the tip of your tongue on the roof of your mouth, behind your teeth.

Focus on the genital or root chakra area and the energy there. Breathe in and imagine that energy rising up your spine, along your back. See that energy come up the back of your head, over the crown and down to where your tongue meets the roof of your mouth. Then breathe out and see the energy continue down the front of your body, and back to your root chakra or genital area.

Repeat this cycle for as many times as is appropriate for you. This could be anywhere from a minute to a 15 or 30 minute process.

In addition to the basic exercise, there are some variations that can be added. You can visualize roots into the ground and branches into the sky and experience the energy circuit as drawing energy up from the earth and down from the sky. You can add in the pelvic rock to this exercise.

Another way to build the energy more strongly is to hold the breath. So, you'd breathe in and hold the breath for several seconds while focusing on the point where the tip of your tongue meets the roof of your mouth. Then breathe out and hold empty, focusing on the root chakra at the bottom.

Tightening the muscles in the genital area on the in breath and holding can help shoot energy up the spine. For this variation, tighten the vaginal muscles and those around the anus while you breathe in. Hold them tight while the breath is full, then release the muscles as you release the breath.

There are many more exercises and techniques for healing and opening to sexuality. For additional resources, please refer to the appendices of this book.

# Chapter 20—Along My Personal Journey

The following are stories and experiences that don't fit readily anywhere else in the book. They include some of my personal journey with sexuality, relationships, and healing.

## Finding soul truth

I recently had the opportunity to explore destiny paths related to my immediate future. A long distance relationship solidified into something wonderful and primary. In that relationship I could see a possible destiny path that led to children, something that I had always assumed would be the road not taken.

So, suddenly I was looking at the element of choice. My love couldn't move to be with me, but I could move to join him. I could choose a child or children and this would draw my energy and attention away from other paths that I had been exploring.

The first part of this journey involved making peace with all the pieces of myself. Because I felt previously that I would choose not to have children, I wasn't allowing space within myself for the part that longed for them. I also got to practice making space for the part of me that wanted a primary, committed partner as well as the part of me that didn't. Once I realized I could allow all these parts to be, without needing to take immediate action, I felt calmer.

Then I started looking at the destiny paths. It had been very painful to get on the plane flying away from this man that I loved. At the same time, changing everything in my life to move to be with him seemed precipitous. I felt like my head and heart had completely different ideas about the right course of action. And, I realized that my struggle about future choices was taking me away from the present moment.

I watched my various stories: "I'm 33, being with him if I decide I want children is a bad idea, I might be too old." "Perhaps he won't love me if we wait." "I'd be vulnerable if I moved, so he would get frustrated with me being unhappy." I found myself spinning in circles.

One day when I was especially wound up about my choices, I did a journey to talk to my guides about destiny paths. They talked about how my focus on marriage and babies with all the conventional trappings was creating that destiny. I had my whole council of guides come in to talk to me about whether that was what I really wanted.

I found that my deep truth was that I did want to be with this man. I didn't know whether I wanted babies, but that was surely an option. In the journey, I talked to my guides about the ways and means of that path unfolding. If I put all my destiny energy into being with him, it would necessarily take that energy away from the shamanic path I walk. That choice was available and honored and not wrong.

And, so I looked inside. I realized that in getting caught up in the newness of this much longed for destiny of a primary partnership with a soul mate, I had lost touch with my passion for my shamanic work. As I explored the question, I remembered when he was in town, how I left to do a talk for a group of people. It allowed me to put the vibrations side by side and note that the feeling of channeling for a group of people and helping them connect to spirit and the feeling of being with my love are both wonderful.

I realized how deeply I want to keep helping people reclaim their pieces and how much I love letting the perfect words to help someone grow and heal come through me. I remembered how I loved doing land healing in Hawaii.

Once I connected to all of this, my guides showed me the destiny path I could create of walking my shamanic path as well as moving forward in the relationship. They told me to do a drawing to remind me of all the passions and loves I have. I also talked to my guides about places I currently spend my energy that I would be willing to give up. I recognized relationships and activities I was willing to release because while they are things I enjoy, they are no longer core to who I am and what I most deeply want.

A friend of mine gave up her job, most material comforts and her sense of financial security to live in Hawaii. I watched her act from this clarity that it was most important to her to live in the place of her choosing and watched the universe align on her behalf. She came back to San Diego, thinking that she would get training and job skills, save money, and prepare to return. I watched her fully commit to that life path and discover her truth again, that she could be living in the most rustic of condition, as long as she was in Hawaii, she would be happy. Not being a rustic conditions kind of girl, myself, I was in awe of her courage and clarity.

Likewise, I love watching my sister's life unfold. She lives in absolute clarity about what she wants and the universe brings it to her. The woman is utterly fearless about challenge, in fact, she thrives on it. Along with this willingness to work hard and put her whole heart into things, I watch her require of her world that she be able to have it all-relationship, work, children. She gets it.

For me, creating the destiny path of my choosing has everything to do with holding all of my passions and desires in my heart. Spirit will act on the messages it gets from me, but if I hold only the relationship and not my love for the shamanic work, the manifestation towards the relationship can get out of balance and all the energy can go to that outcome, to the exclusion of other things. It's not that I have to choose between things, only that I need to hold my desire for everything I want to have it all.

With the power of my shamanic abilities I have the ability to turn away from my original soul contracts and take a new path. In fact, my destiny is very much mine to choose. As a result, this experience showed me how important it is to make sure I'm manifesting mindfully, lest I give up things that are important because I don't remember to love what's right in my life instead of just focusing on what I don't have yet.

## Healing Journey

One of my more powerful shamanic healing journeys began in the dreamtime. One of the images that flashed through my dream was having an orgasm and seeing menstrual blood pouring out of me. The image of blood pouring down my legs was repeated later in the day when a friend smudged me with sage. She told me there was a chestnut stallion who was offering his help.

Returning home, I settled in with a breath-work CD and began breathing and releasing. I cried, I kicked, I toned, I sobbed, I shook, I breathed. I cycled the energy up to the central sun to be cleared from my space as I released it. The image of blood flowing from my womb came in again. Then, when that process felt complete, I took a shamanic journey. I found the stallion; I had forgotten about him until that moment. I knew I was to follow him, but every time I got close, he moved further away.

I finally came up to him in a moonscape. I asked what next and he bent down on one knee so I could climb easily on his back. His knee was cut on a rock. I was concerned but he told me it was okay. The blood flowed through the air as though carried by a wind and created a pathway of stepping stones. The stallion walked along the upward, winding path with me on his back. He told me that a blood path was the only way to reach our destination.

We came upon me in a past life. I was struggling to give birth and failing. It was a long, horrible, painful labor. I was dying and the baby with me and in great pain. At that point, I had turned all my power, all my intention inward against my body and the baby. I shredded the energy around the birth and my own womb and ingrained in my own body a deep loathing for being a woman.

There in shamanic reality, with my former self, I was able to hold space for a different outcome. I healed the soul of the child as well as my body in that lifetime. It allowed my former self to actually give birth to the child with ease. When the baby boy was laid in my arms, I (both myself in this lifetime and myself in that other lifetime) began to cry. He was beautiful and perfect. After I'd finished weeping, my former self and the baby went to the light together. Within my current body, I felt self-loathing and body hatred release and flow away. The damage done in that lifetime was cleared away.

I noted how well hidden away that lifetime wound was. The guides said this was because the energy was so powerful, with every ounce of my energy and intention focused on self-destruction. It had been hidden away so that it wouldn't be opened before I was ready and able to heal it. I needed a certain degree of shamanic strength to clear it and it wouldn't have been good for a less experienced healer to have stumbled across it.

The timing was interesting because I had worked that day with a client who had lost a baby that was born to her at 16. She blamed herself for the child's death and it set up a pattern of self-flagellation that resulted in her allowing abuse in her later life.

The night before, I stood naked under the full moon and played with my sexual energy, masturbating outdoors. As the pleasure and power rushed through me, I realized that I had been giving my lovers far too much credit. Not that they weren't wonderful, but I had largely been feeling my own energy in their arms and crediting them with the effect. I realized all this juicy, wonderful, take my breath away energy was my very own. It was me turning myself on and sharing that with others, not them giving me the experience.

Once all those pathways opened, I was able to open and clear this lifetime. My next menstrual flow after this healing was painful. I had severe cramps, released many blood clots and generally felt ill, spacey and exhausted. The physical follows the energetic and with this deep healing to my soul and essence, the physical body was healing and releasing the pain that it remembered from this other lifetime experience. The periods in the months that followed became much easier.

## Men heal from proximity

Somewhere along the way, I suddenly noticed, that both my book and my quest hadn't just been about healing my sexuality or other women's, they were also about the healing that takes place around men's sexuality and intimacy skills.

My goal was to connect to my own sexuality, heal my wounds, feel safe and joyful in that energy when I began my kissing quest. In writing this book, my goals include offering women a viable roadmap for opening to this sacred part of themselves and having fun along the way. I almost missed the collateral healing that takes place in the men.

In the course of the couple of years that I was actively pursuing my kissing quest, I took home much more carefully selected lovers. I was choosy because letting someone touch my body in that way was still rather scary and intense, so I needed to be very sure I was safe. For these casual lovers, I picked men with warm hearts, who responded with great delight and admiration to my sexuality. I initiated relationships with their delighted cooperation.

In each case, I was clear that I wasn't available for monogamy and that I was playing casually. Three of these relationships were with men who had been having long dry spells in regards to being in a sexual relationship. In some cases it had been years. They had good, warm hearts, great love for women, but did not feel that women were very attracted to them and had given up trying to be with women.

I joke, partly tongue in cheek, that I should come with warning labels for my lovers. I have this bright, shiny energy, I'm sensual and sexual, and love having fun. A number of people are drawn to playing with me in one way or another. What they don't realize amid the "ooh, shiny" reaction is what a powerful, life-changing catalyst I can be, whether I'm trying to or not.

Each of these three men had a deep longing to have a primary partner to spend the rest of their lives with. In fact, two of them ended the relationship with me because they wanted more and my casualness didn't feel good after a while. The third was the man who taught me that it isn't enough to have someone I'm really into or someone who's deeply into me emotionally and mentally, but only moderately sexually. Not that he wasn't excited to have sex with me, but this discomfort of knowing I wasn't his type caused me to end the sexual relationship.

We all stayed on good terms, which allowed me to hear about their future dating lives. All three of these men met their soul mate and life partner and were planning a wedding within a year of us parting ways.

What role did spending time with me have in their finding life partners? I'm not sure. Since they don't have my ability to see a pattern, they would probably just remember me fondly and say that the time with me was great, but the long-term love was really what they wanted and was therefore more fulfilling.

My guess is that when I came up to them and said I found them attractive and offered an invitation, it allowed them to feel more confident and raised their self-esteem. Some old wounds with past failures with women seemed to get washed away with the unconditional positive regard I held for them.

In the "Making Sense of Men" seminar I attended, they talked about how men investigate their ability to make a woman happy. Women think men want low maintenance women but actually it seems that men look more for women who receive the things they do and respond with appreciation and happiness. So, where these men had felt they failed again and again with women, they succeeded with me, made me happy, were valued and cherished by me. It healed a wound and left them feeling that they could succeed with a woman.

The most wonderful thing about this was that I didn't have to "do" anything. I was merely clear about my goals, taking good care of myself, asking for what I wanted, playing, growing, learning, healing. I didn't give advice or do soul retrievals or spend hours trying to make them feel better about themselves. I just cared about them, enjoyed them, felt gratitude for the ways they enriched my life and wandered onward to the next experience when that was done. So, as I healed my wounds, a healing naturally seems to have happened in the men whose lives I touched.

I learned that when I smile, touch, cuddle, laugh, and run energy with men, I do well by them. Even in the absence of sex, there is a healing opportunity for both people.

## IN CONCLUSION

As the season turns to fall each year, there is an opportunity to honor what's gone before that has contributed to growth, and to release that which is no longer needed back to life force energy. My friend and fellow shamanic practitioner Mara Clear Spring and I were talking about planning a harvest ritual amid the corn stalks in her garden.

The guides connected us to the metaphor of the corn and cornstalks. Among indigenous, corn-growing cultures, the corn provides food for the present, food for the winter and seeds for the next planting— basically great richness for sustaining life and new growth. The corn husks and stalks serve the purpose of providing everything that the corn needs to grow to the point that it becomes food and seed. In the fall, the stalks and husks have served their purpose. At that point it is appropriate to burn or compost them.

The guides talked about making a ritual of burning the stalks. They said that when the stalks are burned or composted, it's a way of returning them to the cycle of life. The form is changed and they can provide sustenance for new growth. It is appropriate to burn these stalks and husks with mindfulness of honoring what has gone before, the role that they played in the past and the role that they will play in the future.

The guides showed me how we, as humans, often hang onto our corn husks in terms of our experiences. We go through relationships and situations that are growth producing. Even things that are horrible often help us to grow and change and evolve along our soul path. The trouble is, we often hang on to part of the experience that isn't the part that feeds our lives in some fashion.

For example, I found that in one of my past relationships, while I honor the tremendous growth, I was also holding some of the anger about the pain that I experienced and the unfair way I was treated. The energy of that anger was the corn husk that instead of releasing to become new energy, I was carrying around with me. It burdened my energy field and blocked the flow of life force energy. It was good anger at the time I left the relationship, because it told me where my boundaries were being crossed and prompted me to make new, life affirming choices, like leaving. But, years later, it served me best to let go.

Also, as I walk my path, I find that things change. Relationships, activities and ways of spending my time that once provided great fulfillment, now lack the same power to nourish me. I've outgrown certain things and it's necessary to let go and make space for new. For instance, years ago I sang in a Celtic folk band called the Wild Oats. It was wonderful—yet at some point it became less fulfilling and wasn't feeding me in the same way. In releasing that piece of my life, I saw how it had helped me to grow to where I could begin my kissing quest. Now the kissing quest is mostly over (I occasionally make exceptions) and the book is born.

As you come to the end of this book, I and the guides invite you to engage in a ritual of releasing your corn husks. Consider what anger and bitterness you might still be carrying about your past sexual experiences. Consider what relationships or activities might be complete for you. Write about it and find the ways that the experience as a whole helped you to grow, learn, or become stronger. Figure out what piece of the experience serves you in a positive, peaceful way today and affirm that you are keeping that piece. Then burn the writing, asking spirit to help transmute the energy that you carry from the experience that is no longer needed back to universal life force energy. I recommend doing this outside, inviting the harvest goddess to oversee your efforts, and choosing one of the nights close to the full moon. The most important thing is to do this in a way that honors the experiences and things that went before.

I have been extremely blessed on my personal sexual journey. It is my fondest hope that you will find your own journey as powerful, empowering, unique, and fun as mine has been. Whatever use you make of it, I want to thank you for reading my book.

# BIBLIOGRAPHY/RECOMMENDED READING

*Practical Shamanism: A Guide for Walking in Both Worlds*, Katie Weatherup. San Diego: Hands over Heart, 2006.

This is my first book. There are worlds of healing, protection, and insight available to you just beyond ordinary reality. The knowledge to simply, powerfully journey to these worlds, to connect with your spirit guides, to build a vision of yourself as healthy, intuitive and psychically alive, is within this book. Whether you are just beginning to seek a truer and more meaningful existence, or you are an experienced traveler of worlds, this book provides a reliable, straightforward, friendly and practical guide to basic shamanic practices, including more advanced instruction in past life healing, shadow work, and soul retrieval.

*Sacred Travel- Practical Shamanism for Your Vacations and Vision Quests*, Katie Weatherup. San Diego: Hands over Heart, 2013.

*The Dark Side of Light Chasers*, Debbie Ford. New York: Riverhead Books, 1998.

This is the best book I've come across dealing with shadow work

*Journey To Sexual Wholeness: The Six Gateways To Sacred Sexuality*, Kypris Aster Drake. San Diego. Yabyummy Press, 2008

Kypris is a dear friend and tantra teacher in the San Diego area.

*Loving What Is: Four Questions That Can Change Your Life*, Byron Katie and Stephen Mitchell. USA. Three Rivers Press, 2003.

I have found Byron Katie's books tremendously helpful in unwinding my painful thinking.

***When Things Fall Apart: Heart Advice for Difficult Times***, Pema Chodron. USA. Shambhala, 2005.

Pema Chodron's books and CDs, such as this one, provide loving, beautiful instruction on Tonglen. Tonglen is one of the most powerful practices for transmuting painful emotions that I have experienced.

***A Woman's Guide to Opening a Man's Heart***, Kamala Allen, Ph.D. Trafford Publishing, 2008.

A step-by-step guide for creating love's alchemy rather than relying on love's chemistry.

***Anger: Wisdom for Cooling the Flames***, Thich Nhat Hanh. USA. Riverhead Trade, 2002.

This book provides gentle, compassionate, clear and simple instruction for dealing with uncomfortable emotion.

***Shamanic Journeying: A Beginner's Guide***, Sandra Ingerman. Colorado: Sounds True, 2004.

This book covers the basics of shamanic journeying. Sandra Ingerman has also written *Soul Retrieval* and *Welcome Home*, which are excellent books related to soul loss and soul retrieval.

***The Journey to the Sacred Garden: A Guide to Traveling in the Spiritual Realms***, Hank Wesselman. USA: Hay House, 2003.

This book also covers the basics of shamanic journey. In addition, Hank Wesselman deals with how to explore and use your place of power to affect change in your life.

*Shaman, Healer, Sage: How to Heal Yourself and Others with the Energy Medicine of the Americas,* Alberto Villoldo. New York: Harmony Books, 2000.

This book has good information about right alignment and right relationship to the universe.

*Psychic Protection,* Ted Andrews. USA: Dragonhawk Publishing, 1998.

Ted Andrews is one of my favorite authors. His writing is clear, accessible, and filled with compassion. I recommend this book for anyone who is feeling nervous about the unseen world or who is looking for ways to better manage the energy they take in from the world around them.

# Healing Practitioners and Other Resources

In addition to my own services, I highly recommend the following practitioners:

*Mara Clear Spring* is a dear friend, fellow shamanic practitioner, Reiki Master, advanced graduate and co-facilitator of many of my classes. www.maraclearspring.com, 619-972-2469

*Deborah Barry* is a gifted acupuncturist, shamanic practitioner, and Reiki Master and an advanced graduate of mine. 619-469-2027

*Jennifer Masters*, my cover artist, New Moon Design, 619-255-8070, jennifer@new-moon-design.com, and Shamanic Trance Dance facilitator, www.EclecticTradition.com

# Classes and Workshops

I offer a number of workshops and seminars. For the most up to date listings, visit my website at https://handsoverheart.com

*Learn Shamanic Journey*—in this one day class, I teach students to do shamanic journey to meet and connect with their guides.

*Meet your Star Being*—in this 1-2 hour class, experience a guided journey to meet your Star Being, an energetic guide to help you manage energy and awaken your gifts. Meet your Star Being is also available as an .mp3 download.

*Spiral Wisdom*—this six month journey involves in depth shamanic training, Reiki training, and personal healing.

*A Shamanic Experience*—Mara Clear Spring and I lead shamanic retreats in various locations, such as Hawaii.

In addition to my training, I recommend:

*Pax Programs*, www.understandingmen.com—They offer a free seminar "Making Sense of Men" that is excellent.

*Foundation for Shamanic Studies*, www.shamanism.org—The foundation offers excellent shamanic training in locations throughout the world.

# Acknowledgments

I am deeply grateful for many ways that I have been supported on my own personal healing journey as well as the journey to this book, by beings both in physical and nonphysical form. As regards the physical ones…

I am grateful to my wonderful editors and dear friends, Mara Clear Spring and Laura Kate Barrett. Thank you to Jennifer Masters for the lovely cover art and to Laura Kate Barrett for the graphic and text layout.

Thank you to those who helped remedy my various errors of word usage and other copy editing issues: Jo Balmes, Kim Bjarkman, Phil Poisson, Margaret O'Malley, Shirley Shelly, and Kelly Fisher.

I appreciate all the wonderful people who were available to press their lips to mine, and especially those who have been my lovers: alas, it would be indiscrete to mention you by name. Significant friends, teachers, and cheerleaders include Mara Clear Spring, Laura Kate Barrett, Abby Odam, Mellissa Seaman, Deborah Barry, Jo Balmes, Annette Suarez, Donna Tello, Ken Morehouse, my parents- John and Cari Weatherup, my Temple Priestess sisters, my Spiral Wisdom students, and the members of Drafn and Amber Moon.

# About the Author

Katie Weatherup is a shamanic practitioner, a Reiki master, and a former mechanical engineer. Her unique perspective on shamanism centers on the application of each person's spiritual and intuitive abilities to the issues attending everyday life from a pragmatic, "what works" point of view. She helps people find their way back to themselves, all the parts they have lost, forgotten, denied, and disowned. Katie helps people realize new levels of happiness and fulfillment in a single session and to form a direct, personal connection with the divine.

Shamanism is a staple of her healing business, Hands over Heart. Currently residing in San Diego, Katie offers distance healing sessions and soul retrieval to clients all over the world. She also teaches classes in shamanism via her online academy. Katie's "Practical Shamanism Podcast" is available on the major podcast platforms. For more information, visit her website at https://handsoverheart.com.

www.ingramcontent.com/pod-product-compliance
Lightning Source LLC
Chambersburg PA
CBHW051649040426
42446CB00009B/1045

# Praise for Practical Shamanism: A Guide for Walking in Both Worlds

*Practical Shamanism* is an extraordinary tool for growth and self-actualization. It applies the wisdom of traditional, shamanic cultures to a busy, modern lifestyle.

—Michael J Majeski M. Ed., Psy.D.; Clinical Psychologist

Our experience on this Earth can be difficult to say the least. A spirit having a human experience is not easy, nor did we intend it to be. This book holds the key to building the bridge between the spirit and the human. Katie takes shamanism to new levels with her practical and simple approach. This book contains new views and uses of time honored traditions in shamanism.

—Steve Rother, Author, Spiritual Psychology; Lightworker.com

Excellent guide that blends modern views with time-honored shamanic traditions. Written by shamanic practitioner, Reiki master, and mechanical engineer Katie Weatherup, *Practical Shamanism: A Guide for Walking in Both Worlds* is a guide to the metaphysical power of exploring worlds beyond the mundane, building a bond with spirit guides, past-life healing, shadow work, soul-retrieval, and the search for a more meaningful existence. Written to be accessible to readers of all backgrounds, *Practical Shamanism* guides both novices and experienced shamans with sensible advice and provides numerous anecdotes of other individuals' mystic experiences. A bibliography rounds out this excellent guide that blends modern views with time-honored shamanic traditions.

—Midwest Book Review